To Bob
- Love Har
Christ.

THE DAYS OF MY YEARS

CLARE GALVIN

Canadian Cataloguing in Publication Data

Galvin, Clare F.
The days of my years

Some articles previously published in the Peterborough examiner and My town - my memories.
Includes index
ISBN 0-9697063-1-6

1. Galvin, Clare F. 2. Peterborough (Ont.) - Social life and customs. 3. Peterborough (Ont.) - Biography.
4. Irish - Ontario - Peterborough - Biography. I. Title.

FC3099.P48Z49 1997 971.3'67 C97-930479-2
F1059.5.P4G34 1997

Cover and book design: Elizabeth Galvin
Editor: Jean Brien
Design & Production by F.P. Comrie Publications

Printed and bound by Transcontinental Printing Inc., Peterborough, Ont.

Prudence Felicity Publishing Inc.
Ennismore

For Sharon Mary Murphy

and

Alfred William Gariepy

Clare, at the time of his death, was preparing a manuscript for publication. The articles appearing in "The Days of My Years" were first printed in The Peterborough Examiner in the column "Clare Remembers". They come to you now, with my love.

the chatelaine

Other books by Clare Galvin

THE HOLY LAND - A History of Ennismore Township

MY TOWN - MY MEMORIES

ACKNOWLEDGEMENTS

I would like to thank the following people who assisted me in the preparation and publication of THE DAYS OF MY YEARS: Foremost, Elizabeth McNeill Galvin, my wife (often referred to as the chatelaine), for her encouragement and loyalty; Janet Baal, Peterborough Examiner editor; Jean Brien, editor and friend; Pat and Fred Comrie; and the nuns of St. Joseph, who were responsible for my early education, who guided me in the paths of righteousness and sometimes even scored! And for that one aging nun, who accosted me on the street, placed the palm of her hand on my chest and commanded: "Repeat after me. 'It is i before e, except after c, or when used as...', remember now, Clare Francis, don't be bringing shame upon us." And for my more ardent readers who called me, dropped a note or gave me a simple pat on the head, I am pleased to extend my thanks and May God Bless You All.

TABLE OF CONTENTS

PREFACE

In a preface an author is granted lines to help retail his writings; he is expected to make profound comments. I haven't had a profound thought since the demise of Gilligan's Island.

The Days of My Years should appeal to the seasonable mature. Even the younger set might enjoy my mirror of yesterdays. It might just ring a bell. Not a loud alarm, but perhaps the tinkle of the sanctuary bell.

Because many of the articles have appeared in The Peterborough Examiner as an entity, repetition of literary expression will occur.

Toward the volume's end, there are a few tales taken from my previous publication, *My Town - My Memories*, reprinted by popular request (as God is my witness).

Part Four is composed of articles written about Ireland, a land I love and visit every year.

To complete this odyssey is indeed a relief, akin to a long trek through the woods: parting branches, stumbling over rocks, boots stained with moss, stopping to rest, listening to the gossip of crows, catching a glimpse of a cardinal, being chastised by a matched set of blue jays, kneeling by a hidden spring for a refreshing drink of branch water, and just at dusk, catching sight of the lights of home, with the chatelaine and Bonnie Bluebell there waiting for me.

The book is done. FINIS has been etched below the bottom line of the final chapter. I am glad and saddened that it is all over. But in years to come, I can pick up and read *The Days of My Years*, a comfortable pew.

To my appreciative reader, a wish:

May God hold you in the palm of His hand

And never close His fist too tight.

January

1997

C.F.G.

PART ONE

The Condo Consideration

The chatelaine and myself reside in a modest bungalow on the shores of Lake Chemong, on property once owned by my great grandfather, Patrick Gallivan. The house was built 39 years ago with the help of Central Mortgage and Housing.

As I write, the clock shows 4:30 p.m. The day is bitterly cold, minus 23 degrees, and only God knows the windchill factor. I glance out the window and see a scene lifted from Dr. Zhivago. The chatelaine is absent and there is no intelligence posted on the fridge door, so one must conclude she is at large. Not to worry, however; with her Mennonite/United Church background, I find her totally responsible.

I am not alone. Prudence Felicity is stretched horizontal on the rug beside me, fast asleep. Occasionally when the mood is upon her, she will roll on her back with her four feet pointing at the ceiling. I scratch her tummy; she assumes her former position. She is quite ridiculous. I have tried to raise her in a strict Roman Catholic environment, but with the Protestant influence, it is not easy.

Today I am heavy with care. These days we are considering purchasing a condominium. The years have taken their toll; our mutual health is passing fair, but not robust. Since our future domicile will have less footage, it will be necessary to put some of our belongings on the auction block. I just now brewed myself a cup of coffee which I liberally laced with rum; because of the chill in the air and the decisions ahead, I must be fortified.

On my left is a three-foot high, ornately-carved dinner gong. Acquired years ago, it would do justice to a Cistercian monastery or a stage setting of *The King and I.* Of course this must accompany me.

Along one wall, reaching from floor to ceiling, is a wonderful Victorian bookcase where our favourite volumes of art and literature nudge each other. The chatelaine was about to purchase this beauty decades ago from a woman who was migrating to New Zealand. I did not approve and loudly voiced my objections. Months later a local storage firm contacted me and enquired as to when they might deliver our bookcase. When I saw it in place I loved it. But would I give the chatelaine credit for her taste, her wisdom? Not on your life. A man must retain his pride. On occasion I would enter the room, lean against the glorious case, push my glasses still further down on my nose, tuck the palm of my hand inside my jacket, and in a sepulchral voice announce to all and sundry: "Gentlemen, Mr. Lincoln has just died." Then I would hurl my frame on the chesterfield, laughing uproariously. Despite my antics, I can not leave this bookcase behind.

We have an oil painting of a sad but comely Spanish lady. Would you believe she once graced the walls of Batista's Cuban bedroom? When Castro's campfire boys entered the presidential palace with machine guns blazing, Batista made his escape, but "Consuelo" (I have named her) was hit thrice. I rescued her during one memorable trip to Cuba, took her to a local restoration expert skilled in gunshot wounds, and there she hangs, still sad, but looking grand. I could never desert her. There is another oil painting, entitled "*Young Girl at Prayer*". She once hung in the Louvre as part of an amateur exhibition. She goes with us.

Hanging at the hall entrance is a tapestry the chatelaine brought home from Lisbon. It is a copy of Hogarth's "*The Rake's Progress*" and was purchased because she imagined the rake and I bore a striking resemblance.

On a side table is a wood and gesso figure of a saint, 12 inches high, 16th century Spanish. Both arms are missing. Legend has it that on some significant anniversary in long ago times, family members would commission a sculptor to create an icon to honour their parents, the subject perhaps their patron saint. When one parent died, an arm would be severed from the statue and then the other when the remaining parent succumbed. The saint comes along, though I don't imagine that at this point in history he will be too thrilled with the idea of living in a condo.

Over in the corner is a library chair. The chatelaine again hit the auction rooms for this buy, only on this occasion the money used for her purchase had been designated to pay the hydro bill.

"Gladly", a female teddy bear, occupies a small antique chair in the hall. There she has sat for 30 years, wearing her little granny glasses and holding a tiny copy of the poetry of Wordsworth. I would never leave her behind. Besides she has only reached page 23 in her book.

There is a well-executed portrait of the chatelaine that pleasures the front hall. Twice a day I pass it and am reminded of the lines "...That's my last duchess painted on the wall...". The chatelaine was younger then and less attractive. The painting will come, plus the original sitting model.

Above the fireplace is a brass plaque that reads in Celtic: "There is no hearth like one's own hearth." There are so many possessions of no particular earthly value, but each with a place in my heart, a reminder of someone or some place.

Prudence Felicity has just awakened and is staring at me with her gorgeous black eyes. Old "Prue" is aware of everything coming down, and why not? She is the seventh daughter of the seventh daughter and she senses a change.

From my living room window I have witnessed thousands of sunsets and because I am an early riser, a matching number of sunrises. Julia Ward Howe (*The Battle Hymn of the Republic*) also wrote, "*Let us thank the lavish Hand that gives the world beauty to our eyes, and bless the days that saw us young and the years that make us wise.*"

Just imagine the number of picnics we enjoyed lakeside, the number of campfires, fishing from our dock, the boat trips, the cross-country skiing sojourns, our sessions of archery practice, the midnight skinny dips to cool the body and soul, or the times just spent sitting in the sun rediscovering an old favourite book.

My niece was married on that very lawn, walking in her white wedding gown down a path strewn with daisies to pledge her troth under an arch of roses, the prettiest thing in Christendom.

I remember the family parties. I remember our house-warming and our parents commenting on how lucky we were to get such a start in life, new home and all.

Elizabeth Grace, whom I sometimes call "Amazing Grace" and other times simply "the chatelaine", will soon return and I will persuade her to sit down and have a heart-to-heart on the general prospect of the condominium. With my convincing powers and her gentle sway and quiet voice, the decision I know will be "We stay!" At least for a few more years.

Then I will bring in some wood for the fireplace and we will sit and enjoy our very own special hearth, because there will never be another one quite like it in the entire universe. And that I know for certain.

Relaxing at home, with Prudence Felicity.

Secret places where the chub lurk.

The Summer Of Letitia Rose

She was my first date and her name was Letitia Rose Smallpiece, an Ottawa Valley girl spending the summer months with a maiden aunt across the road and down the street. The aunt called my mother: "Would Clare Francis escort Letitia Rose to a movie? She is expiring from boredom." My mother, good Christian soul that she was, offered my charms and social graces such as they were. I resented this. At least Mother could have discussed the whole thing with me, but sometimes I am inclined to 'go on', so Mom, in her wisdom, cut me off at the pass.

I borrowed my brother's Donegal tweed sportcoat, brushed my teeth, shone my shoes, straightened my tie and picked up Letty. She was very plain, very ordinary, with a wealth of freckles. The thought occurred to me that perhaps everyone in the Valley looked like that. Sometimes the water will do it.

The movie was "*The Trail of the Lonesome Pine*" starring Henry Fonda, Sylvia Sydney, Fred McMurray, Nigel Bruce - a story of feuding families, touted as the first techni-color film made outdoors. On the way home I took Letty for a coke at the Paris Café. Suddenly I was having fun. Letty no longer seemed plain and ordinary.

"*Gee it's great, after being out late,*

Walking my baby back home

Arm in arm over meadow and farm,

Walking my baby back home."

I forgot to tell you that Letty had an engaging personality, a composite of the wistfulness of Joan Fontaine and the humour of Carol Burnett, and so I was suspended midair between comedy and high drama.

"*We go along, harmonizing a song,*

Or I'm reciting a poem.

Owls go by and they give me the eye,

Walking my baby back home."

We talked about our aspirations. I was going to join the Royal Canadian Mounted

Police because I was mad about horses. Letty wanted to become a dentist, which I thought was slightly off the wall. (I didn't make my dream, but Letty did.)

"We stop for awhile, she gives me a smile,

And snuggles her head to my chest

We start in to pet, and that's when I get

Her talcum all over my vest."

We went everywhere that short summer: baseball games at Riverside Park, the exhibition, even a religious revival meeting - tent style - in Confederation Square. I took Letty chub fishing in Jackson Creek, because I was the only one who knew the secret pools and she pledged not to talk.

Sometimes, with abandon, she would throw her arm around my neck. Just in comradeship, you understand. In later years, with the older gals, I would encourage such action.

When I ran into the guys I usually hung around with, I was razzed and kidded: "Galvin's got a girlfriend! Galvin's got a girl!" Before the year's end they followed my lead.

Then came one Saturday morning when Letty appeared on our back verandah. She had come to say goodbye. Her mother was ill; nothing life-threatening, but she needed Letty at home.

Now you are not going to believe this, but Letitia Rose suddenly threw her arms around me and kissed me square on the mouth, right in front of my mother. Then she was gone. I glanced at Mom. She said: "I like that girl, but she seems a trifle fast." So ended the summer of my content,

The years passed. Occasionally I would receive a postcard from some exotic place where Letty was attending a dental convention (because the practice of dentistry is an exotic profession). Three years ago, just before Christmas, the telephone rang and I was speaking to Letty herself, after half a century. I asked: Could I take her to lunch? For a drink? Could she come out to the house? Negative. She was driving from Toronto to Ottawa, accompanied by three grandchildren. The purpose of her call was to determine whether or not I was still answering the roll call, and whether or not the chub fishing in Jackson Creek was still colossal.

Well, we will meet again, perhaps some sunny day, and I will take Letty fishing. I must find out where the chub are lurking. I think I still remember. If not, I bet Letty will.

"After I kinda straighten my tie,

She has to borrow my comb.

One kiss then, I continue again,

Walking my baby back home."

A monsoon coming?

An Essay On Confronting Monsoons

The time is exactly five a.m. I was awakened from a sound sleep by rain hammering on my windowpane. I know the symptoms - a monsoon is approaching. With most people, rain has a salutary effect - refreshing, nourishing, a healing balm. Not so with the likes of myself, and that is because I am always expecting the arrival of a monsoon. The academics say that a monsoon is a seasonal wind of the Indian Ocean, blowing from the southwest from April to October, and from the northeast during the remainder of the year, bringing torrential rains as it blows from the southwest. But what do the experts know? They are forever "carving claims in sand".

One must always be aware of the inherent power of the elements. I am, and I pride myself on that score. At this very moment, I am alert to danger. I shall get all the stuff out of the basement and prepare for evacuation, fill the picnic basket with liverwurst sandwiches, Velveeta cheese, bread and butter pickles, raisin bread, butter tarts and don't forget the tea bags.

The rain is lashing the dining room window now. No question it's a 14-carat monsoon. Being perpetually on the edge of a nervous breakdown, this should be a downer for me. Despite all that, it is now wonderfully exciting. Lightning illuminates the sky in jagged tails; the thunder sounds like pealing from the Vatican. If I survive this night, I will have lightning rods installed on the roof, just like our old homestead. As my sainted paternal grandmother said: "In time of peace, prepare for war." If my own mother were here she would be busy about the domicile sprinkling holy water. My Bichon, Prudence Felicity, just did a walk-on, her tiny white face etched in terror. She shares my fear of monsoons. Because of her advanced years and my concern for her peace of mind, I lift her gently onto the chesterfield and cover her head with an afghan. Minutes later, I hear the sound of her snores. She knows that if I am in the neighbourhood, the world is safe.

Hot damn. I am probably the only person in the parish aware of the impending disaster. The rain continues to lash. With the brilliance of the lightning, I can easily read St. Paul's letter to the Corinthians (I always keep a copy at hand).

The situation is worsening. Should I alert the immediate family? Certainly not before 9 a.m. The immediate are very sticky about certain aspects of protocol.

I am doing my scribbling on the dining room table. The table is a total mess: reference books scattered about, rejected manuscripts, things I created after an unfortunate martini when my mind laid claim to the length and breadth of a living Hemingway. What a mess!

I do have a proper desk, but it is situated in a spot where I can't keep an eye on things. So I sit here, keeping one eye on the spectacle outside, thinking about life, about death and, in this case, about survival. Of late my health has been less than robust. I have attended at St. Joseph's Hospital for tests, but with such frequency that a waggish nun told me my name had been submitted as a possible replacement for the Mother Superior. I readily admit to an air of sanctity about my person and with my recent weight loss, an ethereal quality has been added. I emerge a tall, spare, saintly figure of a man. So much for my grandmother who said I would never amoung to anything. My physician assures me that all tests are negative and that I am as fit as he. My gawd he looks terrible, the pallor alone! Strange the ideas that you kick around in the middle of a monsoon.

I think about the last rites of Holy Mother the Church. I phone my parish priest and get an answering service. I contact a mortician to tell him that I have elected cremation. (There's always someone on hand in those places. The chatelaine later complimented me on my decision, such an adult approach, no ornate casket needed, a simple pine crate would suffice, something that she could use afterward as a planter for flowers.) I get so carried away in thought that I forget about the monsoon.

The rain has stopped and would you believe the sun is peeking its nose out in the east, and Prudence Felicity is peeking her nose out from under the afghan? It promises to be a good day. I feel good. It is not everyone who can face the terrors of a monsoon with such dignity and aplomb.

I just turned on the TV weather station. Not one single reference to the phenomenon. How could they have missed it? So much for the media.

If you become concerned about a possible monsoon in your area, simply give me a call; the walking authority at your service. But of course, after 9 a.m.

The Last Outhouse In Our Town

Once upon a time, when my heart was young and strong, the knees in good shape, the breath fresh, there lived a man named Jesse Aires. He resided in a modest bungalow on the northwest side of Reid Street, just beyond London Street. He shared this domicile with a woman called Madelaine. Both were veterans of the First World War - Jesse a foot soldier, Madelaine a nurse. One day Maddie confided to me that she and 'the man' had never been formally churched. What matters: there was more love and concern in that tiny house than many people kneeling in the front pews of the cathedral would ever experience.

To augment their modest pension income, they sold live bait. One Wednesday, my half-day off, I dropped in to pick up some worms. At that time in history, I was a bit of a Nimrod. Maddie ladled the creatures from the sink into a glass jar with a perforated lid. As I thanked her and turned to leave she said: "Go into the front room and see Jess - it has been a bad week." The man was lying on a leather divan, clad only in his briefs. His entire body was covered with a yellow ointment and swathed in cheesecloth. His breathing was laboured. You see, Jesse was a victim of a mustard gas attack during that first great conflict.

Mustard gas was a chemical liquid warfare agent introduced by the German High Command during World War I. When the winds favoured the process, it caused burns, blindness and death. Survivors experienced constant difficulty in breathing and, on occasion, dramatic skin eruptions.

Jesse enquired: "Clare, how's the pickerel fishing?" My response was: "Not worth a damn. I haven't had a good feed in a month."

Jesse called out to Maddie: "Put on another plate. Clare will join us for a fish fry."

The prospect of having dinner with the team of them was not particularly appealing. Maddie hadn't washed her hands following the worm transaction, and then there was Jesse with the ointment and the cheesecloth shroud. I visibly paled and begged off with the excuse that the chatelaine was experiencing health problems and I had to attend to her.

There was a unique feature about the Aires property. In their back yard, under a beech tree, rested the last outhouse in our town. It was nicely appointed, painted white, trimmed in green, and surrounded with flowers encouraged by the rich soil. I attended the convenience several times in moments of stress. It was rather a pleasant experience with gentle breezes wafting through the open door and an extended view southward.

On one occasion I encountered a porcupine, a little animal notorious for its habit of chewing the wooden outhouse seat which, of course, made a sandpaper job necessary to maintain human comfort. I mentioned the incident to Maddie who advised: "Oh, that's Harry. Not to worry. He's an old friend."

The shrine was a two-holer, in case company dropped by. Last year's Eaton's catalogue hung from the wall of the little structure, suspended by hook and string. Many of the items were currently available, so you could let your fingers do some shop walking. Propped against the wall was a fly-swatter; next to it a tin of chloride of lime with a scoop. Conveniently placed on a shelf on the right was reading material: a dog-eared copy of National Geographic (October 1936) and a worn volume containing the writings of St. John the Divine. This was not your usual, run-of-the-mill backhouse.

One evening, I caught a glimpse of an early rising moon, scimitar-shaped on a clear horizon. It pleased me.

Then one dark night, our city fathers decided that the backhouse had to go, and proper indoor facilities must be installed. With their limited income this was a financial strain on Jesse and Maddie, and so 'the fathers' devised a plan whereby the changes would be made, and over the years the Aires would pay for the improvements with a modest tax increase. You do not win votes putting the heat on a pair of aging veterans.

Well, these folks are now long gone, the last outhouse in our town is also long gone. Tennyson once wrote: "*The old order changeth, yielding place to new.*" Did God fulfill Himself in some way? I question whether He even cared. But I did. I miss that old outhouse, the gentle breeze, the scimitar moon, the revelations of St. John the Divine, the southerly view.

I even miss Harry, the porcupine.

The Allure And The Lure Of The Hook

The other day I went fishing. It was Monday or it was Tuesday. It was not Wednesday because that was the day I was scheduled for ultrasound, so it must have been Thursday. I also have problems with the months of the year.

I have a friend who is the proprietor of a log mansion ensconced on a 150-acre plot, one half-hour south of Peterborough. The plot also boasts a private pond which is exceedingly well stocked with speckled trout. I made telephone contact: Could I fish the pond? Could I bring a friend? Would he pour a couple of libations if there was a noticeable chill in the air? Would he prepare a modest repast after the expedition? I got an affirmative to the first two requests, but a negative to the latter. Was he not aware the latter was a subterfuge to gain the former?

The laird is a surgeon, a graduate of St. Mike's and claims senior internship at Roosevelt Hospital in New York. He is reasonably competent. I would trust him with my life. In fact I have. His personality is inclined to be abrasive; he yells a lot, but if you can ignore that, he is really a good fellow.

I had chosen as my companion for the day an Irish expatriate, Tyrone County born, and at home in Dublin's fair city for a number of years. He became a radio personality, both there and here, and enlarged his income by teaching English and the dramatic arts. With his wonderful voice he quotes Yeats, Joyce, Shakespeare and other writers unknown to me. He also relates off-beat stories, and so do I, so there is communion. The foregoing would seem to suggest that I have many friends. This is not the case. I can number my friends on the fingers of one hand and I consider myself fortunate.

Pushing, shoving, uttering four-letter words and breathing heavily, we managed to launch the aluminum punt. Once seaborne, we realized that we had forgotten some very necessary equipment and we had to hand-paddle our way back to the dock to pick up the oars. Getting old is not always fun.

I watched with sympathy as my friend affixed a tiny hook and half a worm to his line. It is legend that theatrical people are not overly bright. When I opened my own tackle box, the glitter of jewels arrayed therein was dazzling. It came as a surprise and a shock to me when Irish caught ten trout, while I landed only two.

I was mortified. You see I am almost a pro. I learned to fish in Jackson Park Creek using a sapling rod, a length of butcher's string and a bent pin. When I was a little older I used to fish the pier at the Lansdowne lock bridge, and even today my catches are still talked about. Give me a minute! Occasionally I would wet a line at Young's Point or Gannon's Narrows, and I remember the long summer evenings in a rowboat anchored in front of the cottage on Chemong Lake. When the smelt were running, I joined the guys and we would take off for Port Hope and come home with a barrelful. Don't tell me about fishing. I wrote the book.

On our return to the dock, my friend clumsily crawled out of the boat on his hands and knees. I averted my eyes to avoid his embarrassment. When it was my turn, he returned the courtesy.

As we sat on twin benches cleaning our harvest, the surgeon materialized to advise us on post mortem procedure. I believe his sojourn at Roosevelt Hospital has gone to his head.

On our journey home we pulled curbside to view the rolling hills of Northumberland and Durham. With spring busting out all over, it was a grand sight. How many days like this will I have left? You can't checkmate the calendar.

At the homestead, the chatelaine greeted me with modest fervour but with ecstatic enthusiasm over my share of the catch.

Another friend, a descendant of Etienne Brulé (the man who came to Canada with Samuel de Champlain in 1608, believed to have been the first white man to have viewed Lakes Erie and Superior, and was later murdered by the Hurons) counselled me to bathe the fish in warm water and vinegar to remove the slime. What he failed to tell me was the length of time this should take. So in the belief that if a little is good, more is better, I gave the fish a good overnight soak. The French, like the Irish, only tell you part of the plot. So much for Brulé and his kin.

But back to the occasion. That night I retired early, with the fresh air, the sun and the excitement. As I sat on the edge of the bed in my jams, the door slowly creaked open, and Prudence Felicity entered. She, too, has her theatrical moments. Because of my fondness for her and her advanced years, I lifted her up on the bed, swaddled her with an afghan and sang her a couple of verses of "*The Streets of Laredo*". Before you could touch the top of your hat she was off in canine dreamland, perambulating down the streets of that same western town, with a cowboy all dressed in white linen.

There is a rumour abroad that time spent fishing is not deducted from a man's life span. Tomorrow I will try the pickerel fishing in Lake Chemong. I will ignore the blaze of finery in my fishing box and use a tiny hook and half a worm, because life is a learning experience. And maybe I can checkmate the calendar, for a time anyway, and survive to sing "*The Streets of Laredo*" again, and still again.

Fishing with Jack Ainslie, May 4, 1995.

Good Catch!

Lt. Col. John Melton - W.W.1, greeting Lord Tweedsmuir, at C.P.R. station, Peterborough, May 31, 1938.

My Birthday, My Town -
And John The Baptist

Contrary to physical appearance and local belief, I truly was born in this century. The date was August 29, the feast day of the beheading of John the Baptist. I had no hand in the affair. In truth I was in Omemee at the time. My patron saint is Clare of Assisi, founder of the Franciscan Nuns, appropriately called "the Poor Clares".

I do not labour on my feast day; I declare it a personal holiday and I devote my time to a motor-walking tour of our town. From my lakeside home, I drive along the Chemong Road toward Peterborough, and there she is, nestled among seven hills, like Rome itself.

My first stop is a small frame house on Murray Street where I was born on the kitchen table. Someday it will become a shrine, with pilgrimages, miracles and indulgences. I pass The Mount, the motherhouse of the Sisters of St. Joseph, the order founded in France. What a debt our community owes these women for their contribution in nursing and teaching skills. I wonder when they last welcomed a novice. Vocations of today are different.

I drive down to Crary Park. Del Crary and I grew up together, just three doors apart. He was an accomplished musician, a spirited citizen and the park is a fitting tribute. Then I make my way to both cemeteries, reciting short prayers when I see familiar names. (Actually I prefer Little Lake Cemetery, but because of my persuasion I would need dispensation from my own team, and knowing my parish priest, he would say no, and as an alternative, recommend burial at sea. At the very least.)

I drive along Reid Street and pass the site of the old St. Peter's School, where my uncle, Rev. Father Patrick Galvin, master of six languages, served for a term as principal. My mind goes back to a day in May, 1938, when John Buchan, first Baron Tweedsmuir, then Governor-General of Canada, visited our school. The students lined up outside to greet the visiting dignitary. The baron did not descend from his open touring car; rather he extended greetings from the Crown as he sat. Then feeling magnanimous, he dismissed the assemblage, declaring the remainder of the day a holiday. As we raced away, I heard Sister Mary Garneau comment to Sister Anamadeus: "His Lordship has a lot of gall!" I don't believe Sister Garneau was an active Royalist.

I drive the length of George Street. I pass The Barclay, where I laboured for half a century with modest success, and I look up to the apartment windows above where we lived when we were first married. Great years! I wish I could do it all over again.

I remember stores that once graced this thoroughfare: Treblicocks and Sodens Books, Dicksons Dry Goods, Richard Hall Ltd., Robert Fair Co., Graftons, Metropolitan Store, Schneiders Jewellery, Neill Shoes, Bonds Drugs and also McDermid and Jury, Joplings Meats, Anthony Fruit Store, Kresge's, the old Customs House, Barrie Furs, the Capital Barber Shop. All long gone, but busy, vibrant and alive forever in my memory.

I drive along Hunter Street, On my left, high on a hill, stands St. John's Anglican Church. Though not of that philosophy, I love that church, and I frequently pay a visit to kneel and say a prayer common to all Christians.

I pass the Quaker Oats plant, the largest cereal mill in what was once the British Empire, and I remember how the odour of Puffed Wheat used to linger in the air. I cross Hunter Street bridge, reported in some books of knowledge as the longest span of unsupported concrete in Christendom.

I enter the Village of Ashburnham. In a different era, the natives were fiercely loyal to their "tight little island". I stand on the summit of Armour Hill, overlooking the townsite. "On a clear day you can see forever." I spot the spire of St. Peter's Cathedral, where as a youth I served as an altar attendant - when my heart was young and my soul as clean as the driven snow.

Behind me is the hydraulic lift lock, sometimes referred to as the eighth man-made wonder of the world. One breakdown in 100 years. Personally, I don't trust it. I never believed in the principle.

I drive out Water Street to visit the zoo and view God's other exotic creatures, besides myself. I find the enclosure of the Arctic wolves. They pace up and down on the inside, I pace along on the outside. They communicate their frustration, impatient with their forced confinement.

It is time to go home now. Because of the auspicious nature of the day's occasion, no doubt the chatelaine will have prepared a special repast, perhaps there will be candlelight, maybe even a jug of Niagara's finest. Hang the expense.

Before I enter the homestead, I will sit down by the lake and remind myself that I am glad to be where I am, that I am glad to be me!

And as for you, John the Baptist, I am truly sorry, but remember, I was in Omemee at the time.

Lift Lock, June 1, 1938. *Courtesy of Marlow Banks*

Lift Lock, December 27, 1937. *Courtesy of Marlow Banks*

Tunnel at Lift Lock, May 1938. *Courtesy of Marlow Banks*

Isabella Valancy Crawford gravestone in Little Lake Cemetery, Peterborough.

Cemetery Wanderings

Some of my readers are aware of my penchant for attending wakes.

In alliance with that pursuit, I also frequent cemeteries - my favourite verse is Thomas Gray's "*Elegy Written In A Country Churchyard*".

This interest is not stimulated because I myself am approaching the finishing line; rather, it has always been with me.

When I was a youth, aeons ago, I dated a young lady. She was not of my religious persuasion, but she was wildly attractive. Therefore, I set aside my innate bigotry.

The day was Sunday; the centres of entertainment were all closed. Hoping that she might enjoy an inspirational afternoon, I conducted her on a tour of our local cemeteries. The venture was not a howling success, and despite my dedication, the date was never repeated.

Some few years ago at a school reunion, I met the same lady. Five decades had passed; she was no longer young, but she was still very charming. Between periods of laughter, we discussed our single assignation. She told me that whenever my name had been mentioned in adult company, her mother used to refer to me as "the Dracula of the Kawarthas". Now, reader, I ask you, is that fair?

Of interest: Did you know that the cost of a grave plot is approximately $800? This will accommodate two bodies, stacked if the relationship is sublime and the position comfortable.

Choosing a grave marker is naturally important, but one ought to exercise restraint, harness the ego. Once upon a time, within an arrow shot of the house where I was born, there lived a man whose name conveniently escapes me. Years before his demise, this chap had cause to erect his own impressive tombstone.

Inscribed thereon were his credits, his accomplishments. As time passed, further tributes were added. In order to be interred with all his glories listed, it became necessary to shave the marker and re-inscribe the tablet with additional complimentary notes. As a result the stone became delicately slim, and the wafer blew away in that dreadful storm of 1939. I remember the fury well - everyone suffered; we lost our back porch.

Of interest: Did you know that currently 20 per cent of the electorate are choosing cremation? The Board of Directors of Little Lake Cemetery (always on top of things) is having a columbarium constructed to house the remains of 500 additional souls, thus swelling the ranks of the present 29,000.

In this same cemetery, there is another stone that caught my fancy. It was raised to the memory of a young man who sacrificed his life while serving under Lord Kitchener at Khartoum. He was felled by a musket ball, his body found lying on the ground, his head resting on a flat rock. In tribute, his comrades-in-arms sent the stone home to his family, and it was incorporated into the memorial tombstone.

Just inside the entrance gates to Little Lake Cemetery, on a rise of land slightly to the right, there sits the mausoleum of the Morrow family. William George Morrow was Peterborough's first millionaire, and the benefactor of our City Hall. His portrait adorns the rotunda. I knew this gentleman and he, too, was an honourable man. When W.G. sensed he was about to succumb to the ravages of time and destiny, he commissioned the construction of this tomb. Previously interred family members (I assume, complaining bitterly and rattling about in their caskets) were moved to their new mansion. A family get-together is always barrels of fun, but in this instance, I wonder!

To the east, where the road bends close to the water, in this same hallowed acreage, there is a tall Celtic cross commemorating the final resting place of Isabella Valancy Crawford (1850-1887), considered to be Canada's first great female poet. A book has been published dealing with the life and times of this writer. The author is Elizabeth McNeill Galvin, with whom I share more than a nodding relationship.

Also, west of the gate, mounted on a five-foot stone dais, with wings outspread, stands the black angel, almost life-size (although I must admit that my knowledge of angels is limited). Legend has it that the statue commemorates the death of a 10-year-old girl who was the adoptive child of a military man and his wife, bereft of natural offspring. The chosen youngster told her parents of a visitation by a black angel. Her assertion was that she did not belong to them, but rather to the dark lady. Several weeks later the girl became ill and died, the black angel had embraced her.

A man told me a story. It was late one night and there was a full moon. He happened to be driving by the cemetery when his car engine began over-heating. He stopped to let it cool and decided to take a stroll. He was startled to see flickering lights moving around the black angel and dark robed figures. A Black Mass in progress? He beat more than a hasty retreat.

I only visit the cemetery when the sun is high overhead, not that I am superstitious. It is just that it suits my schedule.

It is wisdom to learn from the mistakes of others, and so my marker will be simplicity itself - a granite obelisk 45 feet in height and discernible from the roadway. If you can't drop in, just wave. I'll know! The inscription will bear my name, date of arrival, departure and my FAX number.

With further thought and discussion it was felt that perhaps the presentation was too humble. The chatelaine suggested an added line, and it was gratefully received. Since my family, and indeed the entire parish are aware of my fondness for that extra highball, the last unnecessary martini, a final line will read (and I am content): "He dwelt among us - but not always."

Movie time - an evening at home.

Movies - Then And Now

All the days of my life I have experienced an absolute passion for movies; even in the worst I can resurrect a modicum of worthiness. Years ago I witnessed a film entitled *Ma and Pa Kettle Meet The Monster From The Black Lagoon*. Of course the monster was a product of a dysfunctional family; in fact so was the entire cast.

Two weeks ago I read in our local newspaper a list of the 10 best movies of the past year. Would you believe I hadn't seen one of them?

Several months ago I joined a video club and concentrated my purchases on the cinema classics of yesterday, and even beyond yesterday. Tonight I watched *How Green Was My Valley* (1941), based on a novel by Richard Llewellyn. It told the story of a Welsh coalminer's family and starred Donald Crisp, Maureen O'Hara, Walter Pidgeon and a youngster, Roddy McDowall. I reflected: Growing up on Murray Street wasn't always fun, but in comparison with this Welsh family, my early life was a piece of cake.

In witnessing the movie, both the chatelaine and myself shed tears. Prudence Felicity leapt up on my knee to lick my face and render solace. Does such tearful reaction smack of immaturity? Not a bit. If you can no longer register emotion, then for the likes of you, the bugles have ceased to blow and you can no longer hear the piper playing his lament.

Another video favourite is Maurice Walsh's *The Quiet Man*. Here we find an American boxer (John Wayne) returning to his native Ireland and winning the respect and friendship of the townfolk. The brashness of Victor McLagen, the flashing eyes, the passion and fierce temper of Maureen O'Hara, the cunning of Barry Fitzgerald-all contributed to a stellar 1952 performance. And who would think of casting that hooligan Ward Bond as the village's parish priest? But it worked. Artist and director John Ford mixed a paint-pot full of colours and characters and hurled it at the sky to produce what to me was a rainbow experience. I commend the rerun.

Harper Lee, to my knowledge, only wrote one novel and that was entitled *To Kill A Mockingbird* - but it hit the silver screen. The setting is the deep south of the United States, long before Martin Luther King had a dream. A lawyer defends a black man wrongfully accused of raping a white woman. As the defence counsel, Gregory Peck plays a sensitive role which in that year (1962) earned him an Oscar. This film teaches morality and empathy, and since viewing it I can say with all honesty that I have never killed a mockingbird.

George Cukor's *My Fair Lady* (1964) is a screen version of the Lerner and Loew musical adaptation of George Bernard Shaw's Pygmalion, with Professor Henry Higgins (Rex Harrison) transforming a guttersnipe Liza Doolittle (Audrey Hepburn) into a regal lady. An entertaining movie, a fine musical, a great play. It is interesting to note that Jeremy Brett, the handsome young man so infatuated with Liza that he spends most of his time outside her domicile singing "On The Street Where You Live", later played the role of Sherlock Holmes on TV. Whenever I think of this movie, I say softly to myself: "The rain in Spain stays mainly on the plain" in an effort to improve my diction.

In 1939 Lawrence Olivier frowned, scoffed and sneered his way through the Emily Bronte gothic *Wuthering Heights*. Though the love of his life (Merle Oberon) had a frozen face that belonged on a Dresden doll, the movie was nonetheless great stuff.

In 1942 Humphrey Bogart played Bogart in the movie entitled Casablanca (ever notice how many stars just play themselves?); and I fell in love with Ingrid Bergman, which necessitated junking Deanna Durbin. A man has to do what a man has to do!

In 1951 Bogart again played the drunken captain of *The African Queen*. Somewhere in East Africa, circa 1914, he rescues spinster Katherine Hepburn from a fate worse than death and eventually when the booze runs out, they play patty fingers together. The dialogue is good, the plot is satisfactory, the acting is superb and what a contrast in style!

Anatomy Of A Murder is set in the upper Michigan peninsula in 1959, with James Stewart playing a lawyer who represents a man charged with murder. Stewart bumbles his way to a trial victory as only Stewart can bumble. He is ably supported by Lee Remick, Ben Gazarra, Arthur O'Connell, George C. Scott and Eve Arden. Stewart's defence plea was "irresistible impulse". On occasion I have used this ploy with the chatelaine. It never worked. Stewart obviously was more adept at bumbling than myself.

Best picture of 1962, *Lawrence of Arabia*, assured the subsequent career of Peter O'Toole. It was skillfully directed by David Lean - and I admire everything Lean puts his hand to, short of Mrs. Lean. This was a real blockbuster, with supporting cast Anthony Quinn, Alex Guinness, Jack Hawkins, Arthur Kennedy, Claude Rains and Omar Sharif. With such a group you could turn *The Bobbsey Twins* into high drama. The underlying message of the film: If you are an Arab, never trust the British.

I have decided that I really must try to see some of this year's best 10, knowing full well that these movies won't hold a candle to the aforementioned, but some recognition is due the new crop of kids.

And concerning the aforementioned: as Julie Andrews (later Baroness Von Trapp) would sing: "These are a few of my favourite things."

Christmas Today And Yesterday

This evening, when I returned home from attending a local bistro, I entered an enchanted cottage. In my absence the house had undergone a transformation: the Christmas tree was artfully decorated and the fireplace was alight and festooned with garlands of greenery and red bows. My gratitude to the chatelaine, Elizabeth.

Our tree is an uncommon Scotch pine; it never sheds and it never grows and the limbs fit in by number. The vision reminded me of Christmases long ago, when Shirley Temple was a crew member of *The Good Ship Lollipop*; when Lamont Cranston, with his hollow laugh shadowed his way through another mystery radio hour; when W.C. Fields lurched a path to stardom; when 100 men and all the guys in my town were head over heels in love with Deanna Durbin. And I was young!

I recall one year when the chatelaine was visiting a terminally-ill family member in Toronto. It was a time of sorrow. To dispel the gloom, I concocted a small jar of martinis and commenced to set up the Christmas tree. I was assisted by Maximilian, our three-pound resident Chihuahua, he of the fierce temper sufficient to intimidate a Jesuit. However, Max was president of my fan club and we understood one another. I saucered a small libation for the tiger to further dispel the gloom. The plan was ill-conceived and badly executed. The tree appeared fuller at the top than at the bottom. At the base it disappeared almost entirely. And I had branches left over.

Fortunately for all concerned, Max and I resurrected ourselves early the next morning and there was plenty of time to correct all faults before the chatelaine put her right foot on the door step. When she arrived, the team of us were jewels of sobriety.

I recall a Christmas, many years ago, when I wanted tube skates so badly I could taste the blades. I got them, but it wasn't until a year later that I got the boots to go with them. On Christmas morning my stocking was stuffed with oranges, apples, horehound and chunks of coal. I never understood why the coal was there and I never inquired; perhaps it was an ancient Celtic custom.

There was always a mystical quality to Christmas Eve. In particular I remember walking home from the glory of midnight Mass, with the snow glistening, the warm yellow lights spilling from the windows of the houses that we passed, looking for that special star in the eastern sky and shouting "Merry Christmas" to everyone we met along the way, even perfect strangers.

We trooped along, seven kids with their parents and I especially remember glancing over my shoulder to see my father holding my mother's hand. Almost home, we encountered an elderly gentleman, a neighbour who lived alone and was not of our church. Despite the hour, my mother invited him in for a cup of tea and a piece of chocolate pie. He accepted.

I was 11 that year. I must have been quite a sight with my leather aviator cap with the ear lugs, knitted mitts on a cord threaded through the sleeves of my Mackinaw jacket, whipcord breeks, high jack boots and a many-coloured scarf at least four feet long, made from yarn ends.

I remember the holidays, that wonderful week between Christmas and the New Year, the horse-drawn sleighs with bells ajingle, frost on my eyelashes, snow forts and a thousand snowballs, divinity fudge, shovelling long walkways for a nickel a throw, racing down the hill on a bobsled, sucking icicles and skating on a free rink. There were endless games of road hockey with my buddies. A puck wasn't necessary, there was always a supply of frozen horse buns. I remember cinnamon toast, hot cocoa, home-made soup, the smell of bread dough rising on the back of the kitchen stove - and the special warmth and comfort of belonging to a big family.

Were times more enjoyable then than they are now? Because of the passing of the years, my Christmases are dwindling, making each one more precious than the last. When the lake freezes over, I intend to skate. I hope I won't tumble and shatter to pieces. Would I appear totally ridiculous if I built a snow fort? I wonder where I could borrow a bobsled. Tomorrow I am going to make cinnamon toast.

The chatelaine and Prudence Felicity have long since retired. It is the witching hour. Time to go to bed. No! I won't! I am going to get a pillow and a blanket and snuggle down on the chesterfield and continue to stare at the magical tree and think about other things and other times when I was young.

Not to sound irresponsible, but at my age I am all powerful. I can do anything I wish.

And reader, if I don't see you before the 25th - the chatelaine, Prudence Felicity and I wish you a safe and happy Christmas and all good things for the coming year.

The Importance Of Growing Old

Yesterday morning very early, I stepped out of the shower and confronted my image in the naked mirror. The reflection was not inspirational, not the stuff about which ballads are written. I comforted myself with the thought that an accredited pathologist would recognize some reusable parts. I have white hair which exaggerates the passage of time. I started turning grey on my honeymoon!

I rise early and watch the sun get its act together. Kipling was wrong; the sun does not come up "like thunder", but rather, like a scarlet resurrection.

In those same early morning hours, I do not feed the birds; instead I feed the squirrels who seem to enjoy my company, or maybe they are simply pandering. Then I prepare breakfast for the chatelaine and Prudence Felicity, both of whom share the same dormitory; but I wait until 9 a.m. to awaken them so it is not an intrusion on their dreams. I am not permitted to vacuum before 8 a.m.

Being a senior carries pluses and minuses. I am not intimidated, as I once was. I consider myself the social equal of the mayor; I do not tug my forelock when I encounter our member of parliament, and my parish priest no longer frightens the hell out of me.

I listen attentively when friends speak; I re-read a chapter in a book that catches my fancy, to double the pleasure and because I now have the time.

Sometimes I pay the price: I visit an old friend suffering from Parkinson's, and I remember when this same chap could almost shatter the four-minute mile. Then another with Alzheimer's, but sadly we can't share our mutual memories. I encounter an old girlfriend on the street. She is no longer competing in the Miss Canada pageant, but I look again and can tell you she is still passing fair.

The turned down radio cautions me of sleeting rain and snow. It doesn't matter; I am not going anywhere. Then Mary Martin enters centre stage singing numbers from South Pacific. All in all I prefer the rain and the sleet; even Rogers and Hammerstein can blow the odd game.

Another gift of advanced maturity, along with the greying locks and lower back pain (the latter I attribute to sitting in damp churches), is the gift of awareness. I take a walk in the woods. Of course I see the trees; but sometimes I run my hand over the bark and feel the roughness. I smell the balsams.

A bluejay from his perch scolds me for trespassing. I admire his plumage, further proof that there is a God above. Only He could design such a handsome thing. A small platoon of chickadees perform a high-wire act. Despite my stealth, a partridge thunders out of a clump of cedars, and I know well enough that he will fly in a semi-circle and I will catch still another glimpse of him.

I see the paw prints of a jack rabbit in the fresh snow, then I glance over my shoulder and see the critter racing away. I wish he hadn't. We might have had a moment together. I meant no harm. To echo Burns: "*I am truly sorry man's dominion, has broken Nature's social union.*"

I look out our window and see a small cavalcade of snow cruisers pass by in tandem, the drivers attired like Martians. And I remember when I rode such a saddle.

I spot a couple of ice boats, sails billowing, silently skimming down the lake. In my next life, I fully intend to try that - along with wind surfing, hang gliding and sky diving.

Hot damn, I just remembered I have to go into town for back X-rays. Not to mind; I will use the parish road to avoid the big hill. The natives know me and my vehicle, and generally keep an eye on me!

The day has gone and I didn't even vacuum, but I did mop the kitchen floor. It is late now, time for bed. I must do a check on 'les girls' to make sure that they are properly swaddled and safe for the night, because they are precious to me. More than that, they don't care a hang how I look when I emerge from my early morning shower. Both are fond of me, and why not? I make their very day begin.

In Praise Of Easter

"In your Easter bonnet, with all the frills upon it,

You'll be the grandest lady in the Easter parade."

Easter, that most important feast day of the calendar of Christendom is celebrated on the first Sunday after the first full moon after the 21st of March - which this year falls on April 16.

The Lenten season is that period of 40 days immediately preceding Easter, and it is marked as a time for humility, sacrifice and renewed devotions. Lent, as it is known, follows Mardigras, or Fat Tuesday, so-called from the French custom of parading a fat ox during the celebration of this day.

On Ash Wednesday, the first day of Lent, the priest would place a thumb-print of ash on your forehead. To preserve the mark, I always washed very carefully around it, so my devotion would be apparent the following day. However, because I am a restless sleeper, I usually tossed away the evidence.

As a Roman Catholic, I was obliged to make my Easter duty, which meant attending the confessional, disclosing my sins and faults, obtaining absolution, and then partaking of Holy Communion. Failure to comply indicated rejection of the teachings of Holy Mother the Church. You could become a pariah and end up standing in purgatory for more time than you could imagine. You must understand that Easter meant much more than technicolour eggs and bunny rabbits.

The paschal season was exciting! Under the inspiration of Sister Teresa Maria, a boys' choir was formed to sing during Holy Week, and there was much vying for a berth. Despite my charming voice, I was denied - a circumstance I attributed to religious discrimination. During this Holy Week, the sisters would march us in close order drill to St. Peter's Cathedral for visitation. If I had a nickel I would light a tiny candle and ask God to preserve my parents, then add a further request for my own soul's salvation. It was rather glorious strolling about in what I thought was total Grace.

"Oh, I could write a sonnet about your Easter bonnet,

And of the girl I'm taking to the Easter parade."

Easter was a time to extend your wardrobe. Perhaps a pair of trousers and a sweater from Grafton's on George Street, maybe a new pair of black Oxfords or Sisman's Scampers from Neill's Shoe Store. It was also the time to get your bike out of the woodshed, wipe it down with a damp cloth, oil the sprockets, inflate the tires with a hand pump, and then set off cruising. Most often I would wheel up to Jackson Park and check out the hobo jungle to make sure the lads were still in residence, sit under the pines, watch the black squirrels running helter-skelter, tune in on the crows gossiping, listen to the creek tumbling along and start to plan my illustrious career. I was twelve that year!

After the 11 a.m. Easter Mass, which ended with a Papal Blessing for the congregation from the Bishop of Rome himself, straight from the Vatican (I always wondered how he managed this), we returned home for mid-day dinner, all nine of us.

My father would review the sermon in the event we had missed the thrust of it. Then, our Easter dinner - tinned fruit cocktail, tiny glasses of tomato juice, ham smeared with maple syrup and cloves, scalloped potatoes, green peas and carrots. Mother bought the theory that carrots improved the eyesight. Well, I'm not denying this, but I know they never improved my foresight. At meal's end, my father always complimented my mother on the excellence of the repast, and then said the bottom half of Grace.

Afterward, everyone migrated to the livingroom and all family members took their turn playing the piano, with the exception of myself. I never played the instrument; I regarded myself more an intellectual.

"On the Avenue, Fifth Avenue, the photographers will snap us

And you'll find that you're in the rotogravure."

So many years ago. My parents are gone, as well as three of my brothers. Every Easter I think of the wonderful times we had together. I deeply resent the fact that family members were taken, because I am an incredibly selfish person. Then "patience to prevent the murmur" tells me that we will meet again, for isn't that what Easter and the Resurrection are all about?

POSTSCRIPT:

The song "*Easter Parade*", was written in 1917 by Irving Berlin under the original title "*Smile And Show Your Dimple*". The 1948 Garland-Astaire movie won no awards, but Berlin was paid $600,000. for his musical contribution at a time when a buck was a buck! Not a bad payday for a tunesmith working out of tinpan alley.

Requiem For Prudence Felicity

It was on the eve of Canada Day, 1995, at exactly 8:35 p.m., that Prudence Felicity died. Old Prue, nudging 14 autumns, was a Bichon Frise - about racoon high, with the courage of a Daniel, fighting weight 26 pounds, white curly hair, startling black eyes. Her tail curved above her backside, and its position was a barometer of her emotions. Topside the world was grand; downside, it was a BAD day at Blackrock.

The Bichon, originally from Spain, found itself associated with the Canary Islands where it had been taken by Spanish sailors. Soon, it would become a favourite of the French Royal Court, as well as the pet of Spanish aristocracy, and in Goya's painting "*The Duchess of Alba*", it is the little dog at the hem of the Duchess' floor-length gown. It also graced the laps of such ladies as Marie Antoinette and Madame Pompadour - some ladies, some laps! Prue was really a bit of a snob, but with such laps she was entitled.

In recent months, she seemed to have difficulty hearing, but she was always tuned-in when I said, in a modulated voice, "Your breakfast is ready." So she chose what she wanted to hear.

The Bichon is reputed to be among the most intelligent in dogdom. Regularly, Prudence Felicity watched the TV news; of course she did not comment, but now and then she sniffed, which in itself was indicative.

Prudence Felicity was not overly affectionate, not a cuddler, but when she bestowed some token of her affection, it was like being given a knighthood.

Christmas was her special time. She never tired of gazing at the illuminated tree and, on the festive morn, when she received her gifts (all loosely wrapped for easy opening), she would attack each one with a vengeance. If it was not edible, she quickly lost interest.

Was she really my dog? Or did she favour the chatelaine? No. She was really mine! She indicated this in privacy. Of course she played it close to the chest as any accomplished politician would do.

Of late, when I would take her for an early morning lark along our road, it became necessary, as we set out, to lift her down the two shallow steps to the patio. Because of the age we shared, the going and coming did not exceed more than 200 feet.

Prudence had a favourite spot to meditate, under a canopy of aged evergreens, a little place where she felt hidden and secure. A month or so ago, we had these evergreens removed and replaced with a flower bed. And so on the night of her death, being a creature of habit, she sought this place of refuge, and stretched out on the flowers. At the time ordained, she got up and walked across the patio to find the chatelaine and lick her hand. Then she hemorrhaged through the mouth and died. I knelt beside her, kissed her, said, "It's okay, Kiddo." But she was gone.

We contacted a young couple who live next door, and they looked after everything. Old Prue was buried the morning of Canada day in a cedar grove on her own property.

I forgot to tell you that in her declining months I would lift her up on the bed, and to soothe her I would sing, "*The Streets of Laredo*", which for some reason, pleased her immensely.

The chatelaine and I erected a tiny marker on her grave. It reads, "*Prudence Felicity, Beloved and Faithful*, 1982 - 1995. *Goodbye, Laredo*."

Goodbye Laredo.

PART TWO

Col. John A. Dewart

In Bridgenorth Cemetery there is a small grey granite stone that reads "*DEWART, JOHN A. 1892-1985*". It is a small simple stone marking the final resting place of this man, but he was far from a simple man.

John A. Dewart was born July 16, 1892, on a farm in Warsaw, Ont., the youngest of a family of eight, and he was born with a thirst for knowledge, both modern and ancient. On attaining his senior matriculation, he secured a teaching position in Niagara Falls, and it was there that he joined the reserve army. In 1916 Dewart enlisted in the permanent forces and served overseas with the Canadian Expeditionary Contingent. He emerged from the First Great War with the rank of captain, bearing the Military Cross and an enviable military record.

In August, 1923, John married Emily Ballard of Madoc, Ont., and from that union two children were born: Murray Gordon and Helen Joyce.

In 1937, as a lieutenant-colonel, he was invited to Buckingham Palace to attend the coronation at Westminster Abbey of George VI and Queen Elizabeth.

The career of this man, this school teacher, this soldier, was destined to include much more. He became the owner of a grain mill; he was also a historian, a sportsman, a raconteur, mayor of the city of Peterborough for four terms, and a world traveller. One time, while travelling abroad, he left his trousers at a hotel in Venice. When he returned home, he telephoned: Yes, indeed, the trousers were there, and they would be mailed to him. Dewart replied: "Don't bother, I will pick them up next year." And he did.

In the mid to latter '30s, when we were recovering from the privations of the Great Depression and leaping on carrousels, John A. was the man who, locally, rained on our parade. In his public speeches, he brought the message of trouble brewing in Europe. Adolph Hitler might appear ridiculous, but he carried panzer divisions in his pockets. As well, Britain had lost its traditional protection - the English Channel no longer a barrier through the advanced technology of air power. Dewart was one of the first to sound the alarm.

Following World War I, John Alexander Dewart maintained his association with the military, as officer in command of our own Prince of Wales Rangers. When World War II became imminent, it was such men as Col. Dewart who constituted our first line of defence. However, at the outbreak of hostilities, this man, although he fulfilled all physical requirements, was denied overseas service because of his age. Local Senator J.J.Duffus lamented the waste: "That such a military talent should be lost to our European brigade...". The following is quoted from a scroll presented to Dewart by the Sergeants' Mess, Prince of Wales Rangers: *"May we express to you our sincere regret that age limitations imposed by National Defence Headquarters prevent you from assuming command of the active battalion, now mobilizing for service in the great cause of freedom, to which you devoted such tireless zeal and energy."*

But Col. Dewart had things to do and places to go. He was appointed staff officer to lead the 9th Infantry Brigade in Kingston, which was comprised of the Princess of Wales Own Regiment, the Stormont Dundas and Glengarry Highlanders, the Midland Regiment, the Hastings-Prince Edward Regiment, the Argyle Light Infantry and our own Prince of Wales Rangers.

A personal aside: Some years ago I was invited to the Dewart home for a social evening. The colonel's daughter Joyce (Mrs. Garth Parnell), had cajoled her father into reciting Robert Burns. With book in hand (which he never consulted) he began, *"Wee sleekit cowran tim'rous beastie..."*. In my school days I had difficulty understanding Burns, but that special evening, the bard came alive and strode around the room, with book in hand.

In 1943, National Defence posted our local regiment, the Prince of Wales Rangers to Prince George, B.C., for additional training and as a safeguard against the possibility of a Japanese shore invasion. Colonel Dewart was there in command.

In 1946, John A. was appointed special returning officer to take the vote of Canadian forces serving in Italy, his office - Rome.

Following the war, during his tenure as mayor of Peterborough, he convinced City Council to pledge $200,000 from the sale of the gas works, as a pledge of faith for the establishment of Trent University. Never forgetting the importance of education, he provided financial assistance to two young women living in rural areas to enable them to attend Peterborough Collegiate and Vocational Institute. Both in subsequent years were chosen head girl.

Col. Dewart inspired the founding of Fairhaven, a home for senior citizens. He was a parishioner of St. Andrew's United Church, a 33-degree Mason, a member of two hunt clubs, a member of the Peterborough Men's Club, of the Peterborough Golf and Country Club and later of the Kawartha Country Club. He was past president of the Rotary Club and of the Canadian Seed Growers' Association. He was the first mayor of Peterborough to wear the official chain of office, donated to our corporation by Gordon Monkman, a close personal friend of John A. Dewart. Later for his achievements, he was awarded an honorary doctorate from Trent University.

Those who once brushed shoulders with Col. Dewart might ask: "What manner of man was this?" To everyone he was something else; in truth he was "A Man for All Seasons." For me, he will always remain: Robbie Burns, with book in hand.

P.S.: I feel a sense of obligation to report the names of John A. Dewart's grandchildren of whom he would be immensely proud: John McLean Dewart, Graeme Gordon Dewart, Robert Edward Dewart and Scott Andrew Dewart; Jennifer Lee Parnell, Michael Garth Parnell and Murray Dewart Parnell.

Col. John A. Dewart

The Bugle And The Tam

A brief History of the Royal Canadian Legion

The date is Nov. 11; I attend the Cenotaph service; the mist promises rain. On the fringe of the crowd stands a young lady I estimate to be about a dozen years. Her attire, a navy jumper, a white blouse and crowning her head, her grandfather's military tam with a tuck in the back but the badge intact. She never knew her grandfather. I did, and he was a good man.

The time has arrived. A thoughtful sexton leans against the ropes and the church bells ring out their requiem. The padre approaches the podium, the honour guard is at attention, the bugle plays the The Last Post, and for two minutes, silence falls over the land. We reflect on the sacrifice they made for us. May God have mercy on their immortal souls.

After the service, I attend the Legion Hall in the role of an affiliate member. The atmosphere is subdued, perhaps we can still hear the notes of the bugle resounding in our ears. Later, the glasses will tinkle in comradeship, and stories will be told and retold. The rain is beating a tattoo on the windows. I wonder if the young girl in the blue jumper and military tam with the tuck in the back will get home without being soaked. I could have driven her home, but one doesn't do that sort of thing any more, and that is a shame. I knew her grandfather, a good man indeed.

The year was 1916, late autumn. Some of our soldiers were returning home from World War I, *the war to end all wars*. They formed a club "The Great War Veterans Association". These men had much in common. They shared the same nightmares: the trenches, the mud, the rats, the darkened night skies illuminated by enemy artillery, the crack of a sniper's rifle if a head appeared above the parapet, and the constant fear of the Germans releasing poison gas. Wind permitting, it would not kill but you would never breathe the same again. Misinformation filtering through, "We are winning!" "We are losing!" "The left flank is faltering...". And your reward at day's end, a tin of bully beef. The ominous command come morning, "Let's go lads!"

At the club, you could rub shoulders with comrades who knew what you were and where you were coming from. It was therapy.

When I was a tad, we had a large book, a graphic pictorial account of World War I. Some of the scenes were so horrific, my mother would not let me see, and she hid it. Did you ever try to conceal something from a table-high menace. By eventide, I had it in hand. The tombs of the pharaohs could not conceal their secrets with a kid like me in the parish.

Club accommodation was arranged at Victoria Hall, 332 1/2 George St. N., second floor, above the Deluxe Restaurant and Joplings Meats. Still later, the Barrie building. Following Armistice and the resultant demobilization, larger premises were imperative. With a $10,000 loan from the city, the vacant Murray Street Baptist Church was purchased. The faithful Baptist congregation had built an imposing temple a couple of lance-throws further east.

Eventually the need arose to co-ordinate the existing clubs across the dominion. The result - "The Great War Veterans Association."

In 1920, Peterborough was chosen as the site of the Provincial G.W.V.A. convention. Our town had rail access between Toronto and Montreal with connections to New York and Chicago, municipally-owned utilities, our own Sweet Afton - the Otonabee River - that same river part of the Trent Canal System, the sheer wonder of the hydraulic lift lock, an astonishing industrial growth, and a 10-year population expansion of 70 per cent. Peterborough was a natural choice, a toddling town, this Electric City.

In 1926, as a result of unity meetings throughout the Dominion, the Great War Veterans Association became the Canadian Legion. In 1961, our present Queen Elizabeth II added the title "Royal".

Early in September, 1939, the Second World War began with Axis powers opposing the Allies in the greatest confrontation our globe has ever witnessed. When this war came to an end in 1945, and service men returned home, the ranks of the Legion swelled.

The Elizabeth Smellie Chapter was granted its charter in 1947, its membership open to those women who had served. At the time of this writing they number 100. Though their meeting room is separate, they work with their male counterparts and members of the women's auxiliary on charitable and social projects.

A symbol of the Legion is the blood red poppy of Flanders, immortalized as an emblem of sacrifice and remembrance in honour of the thousands who gave their lives for those ideals which we, as Canadians, cherish. The reader, with permission, may visit the Trophy Room at the Legion, which contains memorabilia from both wars.

Our local Legion, numbering 1400, including associate members, constantly promotes unity of all who served their country and perpetuates the memory of the fallen. It is through the Legion that the voices of all veterans are heard by both provincial and federal governments. It is through the Legion that care and financial assistance are extended to veterans and their dependents in need, with immediate financial assistance in emergency situations.

The pledge and motto of the Royal Canadian Legion reads "Memoriam Eorum Retinebimus" (We will remember them). And we will, so long as poppies grow in Flanders fields, the bugle sounds "The Last Post", church bells play their lament, and a young lady pays tribute to a grandfather she never knew!

Life members of The Royal Canadian Legion, Branch 052, Command - Ontario, are: AGGAS, William; BARTLEY, Donald S.; BASCIANO, Tony; BASCIANO, Patricia A.; BROWN, Keith; CANDEN, T.R.; CONROY, John; CORBETT, Albert E.; CROUGH, Kenneth R.; DAVIS, Harold R.; DAWSON, J. Brenton; DRURY, James E.; DURKIN, L.T.; EANO, Jack F.; EDGERTON, David R.; FOSTER, George B.; GOLDING, Alan R.; HOGG, Eric F.; HOLLAND, Harold; KELCEY, Francis R.; LAWLOR, Frank J.; LEE, Gordon; MOHER, Daisy W.; NICHOLS, Edward M.; PARSONS, Sid W.; PRYSKY, Henry J.; REID, Barry W.; SHINE, Leo T.; SMITH, Wallace C.; SMITH, Viola I.; STURGEON, H.; SULLIVAN, M.D.; and WELCH, Leonard W.

Dr. and Ada Calvert at the Military Ball in Belleville, 1983.

Capt. Leslie John Calvert

On a bright day in May, 1944, on Italian turf, Viscount Alexander of Tunis pinned the Military Cross on the tunic of Capt. Leslie John Calvert, CAMC. The citation reads: *"During the period 20 to 24 May, 1944, the 4th Canadian Reconnaissance Regiment (4th Princess Louise Dragoon Guards) were in Action against the Adolph Hitler Line south of Pontecorvo in Italy. Capt. Calvert was the medical officer attached to this unit. Whenever an attack was in progress and our troops were actively engaged in combat with the enemy, Capt. Calvert insisted on working in the most forward areas. On many occasions he went beyond our front line defences to attend to the wounded without waiting for them to be brought in. This medical officer worked with skill and coolness in many cases under direct small arms fire and under heavy mortar and artillery fire. With complete disregard for his own safety he eased the pain of the wounded. Throughout the entire operation he set an example of courage and devotion to duty which inspired and encouraged every man in the unit."*

Toronto born Leslie John attended Vaughan Collegiate and graduated from the University of Western Ontario. He interned at Toronto's St. Michael's Hospital, then joined the Canadian Army Medical Corps. After the armistice, Dr. Calvert resumed his studies, participating in a demanding course in surgery and specializing in urology with post-graduate work at St. Mike's, Christie Street, Toronto General and Toronto Western Hospitals.

Always a scholar, Calvert was the first part-time student at Trent University, achieving an Honours Bachelor of Arts in History and German. Far and wide he has been acknowledged as an authority on the American Civil War. As a member of the Military Institute, he enlarged his knowledge of this area of history.

Dr. Calvert retired from our local militia with the rank of lieutenant-colonel. He has been a member of several clubs and organizations, a stamp collector and an ardent sportsman. Leslie John served on many local hospital committees and was president of the Peterborough County Medical Society. He also served for six years as Canadian Surgeon General of the St. John's Ambulance Corps, and was instrumental in formulating the revised standard First Aid Manual.

A soldier, a healer, an historian and always a student and collector of knowledge, Dr. Leslie John Calvert is another "Man of All Seasons", but there was a season in early 1944 when, just south of Pontecorvo in Italy, facing the Hitler line, there strode a man.

Alice and Bernie Morin

Romance Amid Chaos

War is a conflict between nations, carried on by force of arms. (Webster, at times, can be simplistic). It is an indescribable and revolting horror that leaves a terrible fear that it could happen again. Sometimes, even in chaos, something shining and bright can happen. Let me introduce two people who shared such an experience.

Sergeant Bernard Morin, regimental number C11447, a member of the Royal Canadian Army Service Corps, 52nd Company, enlisted Sept. 4, 1939, sailed to the British Isles, and arrived in Glasgow in January, 1940. He was stationed at Aldershot, then served in Italy and North Africa before returning to a final posting at Ifield in England, just three miles from Gatwick airport.

The Canadian Army Service Corps was responsible for the movement of ammunition, petrol and food to units of the First Canadian Division.

The history of the Morin family reads like history itself. Noel Morin emigrated from France to New France in the year 1632. He was employed by Samuel de Champlain as a wheelwright, an occupation of skill. Noel was the father of Germain Morin, the first Catholic priest to be ordained in the new land. Noel's daughter, Maria, was the first nun, and she later became mother superior of Montreal's Hotel Dieu. An extension of the family was Etienne Brulé, an interpreter of the Indian language and an explorer, said to be the first white man to view Lake Erie and Lake Superior. Etienne Brulé was a victim of cannibalism by the Hurons for some unspecified crime. One writer labelled him "the immortal scoundrel". But remember, we can't all behave like priests and nuns; otherwise the atmosphere could become stuffy.

Now, entering from stage left, the female protagonist, Sgt.Alice Elizabeth Pruner, Canadian Women's Army Corps, who had arrived overseas in 1942. Alice E. was attached to the Canadian Military Headquarters and billeted in the home of Lord and Lady Abercrombie, 38 South St. in London. I suspect the amenities of these digs surpassed what was offered by the local barracks. Bernard and Alice renewed their Canadian romance and whenever possible synchronized their leave.

Both young people experienced England's bombing. Alice, in London, was among the first to witness the Buzz bombs trailing their erratic course across the sky. One evening, during a raid, two 1000 pound bombs fell near the building where Bernie was billeted. They did not explode. Later the Bomb Disposal Squad arrived and determined the bombs were duds. Inside each one was a note that read: "Czechs - we are your friends."

In these war years it was not easy for two service people to marry. Permission had to be obtained through military authorities, and they could be tougher than Mom! Divine providence prevailed; the two sergeants were united in holy matrimony at St. Margaret's Church in Ifield; Alice E. attired in a wedding gown her mother had made and sent to her. The bridesmaid was Irene Vivash, a friend from Peterborough, Ont., who was also serving overseas.

The best man was Earl Hewitt, a relative of Foster Hewitt. The wedding of Bernard Morin and Alice Elizabeth Pruner on May 1, 1943, was the first all-Canadian service marriage in World War II.

The commanding officer at Ifield, himself a musician, formed a 12-piece orchestra called the "Rhythm Rascals". The vocalist was Bernard Morin. When Bernie returned home he was the featured singer with the Del Crary Band, which played at the Kawartha Room of the Empress Hotel on Charlotte Street.

Sgt. Bernie Morin of the Royal Canadian Ary Corps and his wife, Sgt. Alice E. of headquarters staff, now boast three sons, six grandchildren and five great-grandchildren. Didn't I promise you at the beginning that, even in chaos, something shining and bright can happen? It did. And only three miles from Gatwick Airport.

PART THREE

Meet Bonnie Bluebell

I told you earlier that our dog Prudence Felicity was buried on Canada Day. After that, a kind of hush fell over our world.

Well the chatelaine and himself, being senior citizens, could hardly countenance becoming the owners of a young pup. It wouldn't be fair all around. Hence we obtained an older dog, seven years old to be exact, and once again we share our lives with a Bichon, a tiny lass who responds to the name of Bonnie Bluebell.

She had mothered three litters, a kennel dog, a commercial enterprise, not house-broken, not exactly a Rhodes scholar. Her owner recommended that we purchase a portable kennel, pink in colour and of a specific make. This we did. Bonnie B. entered it once, looked around and since then has never crossed the threshold. She is now a free spirit, doing things she has never done before and "walking down a strange new street."

We wondered how to expedite the house training. No problem. Being a product of the separate school system, I am tremendously creative. I called a neighbour lady. Would she bring over her team of dogs to piddle on our lawn? Give Bonnie a sense of direction. She arrived with Muffin and Sahara, the first a Lhasa Apso, the second a Siberian. What a pair! What a vaudeville act! When the deed was done, I offered my thanks and reimbursement to the lady. Her response was: "Not a bit; it's on the house. Or I should say: It's on the lawn!"

Did the grand scheme work? No it didn't. To be honest, I always had reservations about the separate school system. So Bonnie makes the odd mistake and is scolded sufficiently to experience what we refer to as "the burning shame".

On our early morning walks along the road, everything fascinates Bonnie Bluebell: the cedar rail fences, the black squirrel running atop same, a poplar tree whispering, catching her attention. She restores my sense of observation. That fence line has been there all the days of my life and I recognize that black squirrel; he has a white spot on his thigh. And the sound from the poplars - I remember my grandmother telling me that the cross upon which Jesus was crucified was constructed from wood of that special tree, and that is why the leaves are forever restless.

I glance down at Bonnie's tousled head, and she reminds me of Phyllis Diller on a bad night, or even a good night for that matter. We walk along and I say: "Come on honey, go bathrooms." I think I'm losing it! Tonight I will re-read James Overstreet's *"The Mature Mind"*.

Yesterday morning, after the lark, I cooked some bacon in the micro, and gave Bonnie Bluebell a rasher, her first. She sniffed, tasted, chewed, swallowed and commenced to dance up and down on her bare feet. How ridiculous! When I am so delighted, I at least confine myself to the soft-shoe.

On Tuesday, as needs be, the chatelaine went into town. Suddenly she was missed. The Bonnie raced about checking rooms, closets, opening drawers, to no avail. Finally the little creature, totally exhausted, climbed up beside me on the chesterfield. Not a great alternative, but in times of a storm, a port is a port.

Give me three months with Bonnie Bluebell and she will have her grade six in piano, and be operating the computer as well. In the interim, I hope I can manage to teach her some proper bathroom habits.

We haven't forgotten our old friend, Prudence Felicity, and frequently the hush falls - but it is becoming less audible.

Meet Bonnie Bluebell.

The School Reunion

"With the garnet and grey

We will top each fray

Bear it on, supreme above,

May it never fall

While yet we call

PCI the school we love."

These are the opening lines of a school song, purportedly penned by local barrister James B. Lillico.

On a recent Saturday evening, I attended the Classes of the Forties PCVS reunion. My gawd, half a century has passed and I scarcely noticed. The social was held at the Holiday Inn; you know the spot overlooking the river, a comfortable hostelry, indoor washrooms and all.

At this public high school, I enjoyed a distinction: I was the singular male Roman Catholic in the academic section. Why did I leave St. Peter's? Well, at the time, in my youthful opinion, that institution had some shorts. For example, no gymnasium! You see, I aspired to becoming a professional basketball player, a legend in my own time. And do you know what? I never even made the junior high school team. But dreams are made of fragile stuff. When I made the decision to move, my mother just about had a stroke. My father, a calmer voice, assured her that I merely wished to change schools, I was not on the brink of moral destruction.

Of course I kept my links with Holy Mother the Church. One morning, after assisting at Mass, the rector (a rather corpulent figure, flushed of face - the type RKO films are wont to portray as typical) invited me to breakfast. I knew his intent. So after the repast and over tea, his opening sally was: "How are they treating you at that school?" My response: "With deference". His response: "Then rip into it, Lad, and milk the cow with three hands!"

But back to the reunion. James Swanston ably chairs the head table, flanked by

Arnold Noftall, John Londerville, Mary Overend O'Brien and Bev Goulding. I have been chosen to ask the blessing, not because of my eloquence, but because I appear as a tall, saintly figure of a man.

Across the room, I notice three ladies sitting together, and I remember how I once lusted after their frames. Nothing ever came of this, a tribute to their integrity, or my lack of initiative.

To the left I see Judge Samuel Murphy "who metes and doles unequal laws onto a savage race." Near the entrance is one of Canada's most eminent neurologists, Dr. Joseph Marotto. He is not a grad, but his wife Margaret (Peg) Hughes is. In front of the windows I can see James Hooper, long time City engineer. He knows our town almost as well as I do.

And there is Gerry O'Reilly and his wife Mary Stewart. Gerry was a great lacrosse player. Remember him? Faces pass by, people I haven't seen in years: Bill Patterson, Gary Braund, Barb and Lloyd Routly, Jan Langley Griffin and Dan, who now live in Bancroft, Terry Hill, Mary Patton, who helped make this evening a reality, along with committee members, Marney Hollingsworth Wyatt, Mary Braund Lowes and Bev Brooks Hamblin.

We are seated at a table with Joyce Dewart Parnell and her husband Garth. Garth was responsible for the last PCI Classes of the '40s Reunion held five years ago. Also at our table is Alex McLeod and Mrs. McLeod. Alex was a thrust in the militia. My gawd, his hair is grey! I'm glad it didn't happen to me.

Clumps of garnet and grey balloons bob on the walls of the crowded room. I don't know how many people are here, several hundred, maybe. I'm not good at judging numbers. There is Ruth Telford. We used to date way back then, but she yawned a lot, a condition I attributed to low blood sugar. The bar is actively attended, perhaps due to nerves. As a matter of fact I tried one myself, or was it two or possibly three.

Over in the corner, I see two old friends chatting and I am reminded of a sideline enterprise they both had going for them back in the '50s. Without animosity, one operated a speakeasy in the north end of Peterborough, while the other did business in the south end. Sometimes it was "eat-in", but mostly, it was "take-out". In the war years, during the '40s, every adult was allowed a 26-oz. bottle of liquor a month. Permits were issued for this purpose, and all availed themselves of the opportunity, if only for the convenience of their friends. At the same time in Quebec the allotment was a 40-ouncer. (Even then the distinct society was recognized and observed).

We did not stay for dinner. I was emotionally drained and in addition we had a sick dog lurching about the house. On the way home the chatelaine handled the wheel while I gazed out the window at a darkened sky. Was it the time of day, the season of the year that saddened me, or was it the fact that all those people who once thronged the halls of Peterborough Collegiate Institute were growing old?

Well, in any case, five years down the road, I will again attend the reunion (God being willing and compassionate), and I will look forward to seeing those same faces. The social is always held at the Holiday Inn. You know the spot; it overlooks the river.

1940 - Class 9G P.C.V.S.

Girls sitting, left to right: Wilene Hope, ------, Geraldine Milton, Gloria Lowney, Ruth Florence, Lila Milburn.

Girls standing, left to right: Vivian Martin, Joan Leslie, Lenore Mather, Adele Fitzgerald, Maxine Kidd, June Moore, Theresa De La Plante, Doris Moncrief, Dorothy Larmer, Betty Mantel, Lois Humphries, Monica Lawless, Bernice Harding, Jean Metcalfe, Jean Ferguson, Caroline McCabe.

Boys standing, left to right: Bill Edgar, John Edminson, Arthur Smoke, Tom McCullough, John Hinton, George Gray, Arthur Gertley, Earl Moorehead, George Green, Allan Hooper, Ralph Hall, Weldon Fanning, Clare Galvin.

Saturday morning Irish breakfast club, with niece Sharon Murphy, Frank McCarthy and Stan McBride

Clare's 60th Birthday with friends Gordon Farquharson, John Corkery at Norm Mutter's.

The Story Of A Violin

More than two decades ago, according to the Augustine calendar, a tall spare man entered my shop to purchase a blazer and grey flannels. His grandchild was to be married a fortnight hence. He was old (about my age today), and he had worked with my father at the Quaker Oats mill. A selection was made, but there was one stipulation to the purchase. Could he make monthly payments? Although this was not the policy of The Barclay, an exception was made. The payments arrived faithfully in the mail. Then one morning, the gentleman appeared in person with a proposition. In lieu of his account balance, would I accept a violin of some 300 years' vintage?

I was intrigued and I agreed. When the man left the store, I telephoned a chap I had heard was an authority on stringed musical instruments. When he heard who owned the violin he said: "Grab it. He has another one that is 400 years old."

The following morning the tall gentleman arrived with violin case in hand. I examined the relic, faded wood, worn, rather pathetic (looking much like myself should I live so long). I asked the spare man if he would play a number for me. He agreed reluctantly, saying that he was not a skilled musician. What he played was *"Lara's Theme"*.

Commerce came to a halt; my customers were transfixed. When he finally put down the instrument, I asked: "What is that melody?" He responded: "I don't know. I heard it on the radio. It's a pretty tune." And pretty it was indeed!

The violin appeared to me to be in such poor condition that I decided to take it to a furniture repair man for refinishing. He did a good job. We were both pleased. Then one day, the stringed instrument specialist arrived on the scene. I proudly handed him the shiny wonder.

"My God", he said. "What have you done to it?" When I told him that I had had it refinished, I thought he was going to hit me. He spun on his heels, headed for the door, yelling over his shoulder: "You idiot!"

A month or so ago, I asked Wes Lee, a local musician of considerable talent who hallows old violins, if he would restring the instrument. Last Thursday Wes called me. We would meet the next morning at the Honky Tonk Restaurant in Bridgenorth. He was bringing two friends with him - George Lindsay and Stewart McCue. A mini concert was about to happen. A violin had been restored to life.

I was excited and immediately called several friends to come along. What a great experience! In the hands of Wes Lee, the 300-year-old lady sang and cavorted. For almost two hours, request upon request was performed; Wes with the violin, George and his harmonica and Stew with his guitar.

That evening, I carefully wiped off the aged instrument, covered her with a cloth and tucked her into her case. This was done gently. At her age, together with the excitement of the day, the old lady might collapse and crumble.

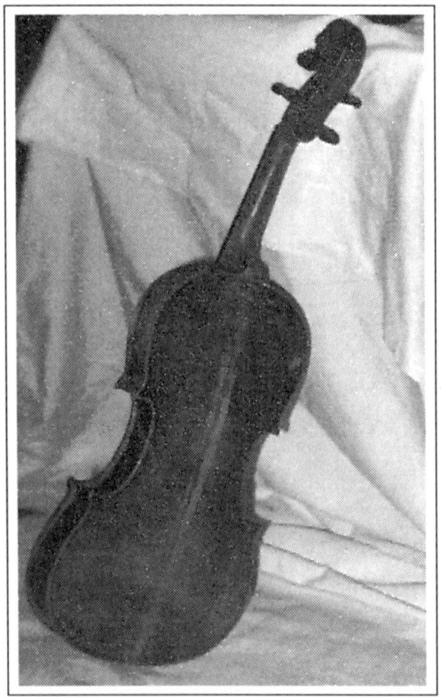

How it arrived.

What I did to it.

Friendship

It is early Sunday morning. Sometime during the night there has been freezing rain. Now as I glance out the window, what I see is spectacular, every tree a mass of glistening crystals, each one artfully crafted by Tiffany's of New York - or was God just having fun?

Since I am in my declining years, it behooves me to comment on diverse subjects. The topic today is *Friendship*. On this score the chatelaine is deserving of the brass ring. Each year she meets with five other gals who all attended kindergarten together. This yearly reunion involves hitting the theatre circuit in exotic places such as Toronto and Niagara-on-the-Lake, midnight dinners and sipping ice wine - the devils! I pray this get-together continues. In between times, there are letters, postcards and a charge of telephone calls.

But back to myself, the hero of this article. I take great pride in having four special friends. Of course I have other friends whose company I enjoy, and I would be saddened by any loss in the ranks.

The Irish Club meets every Saturday morning for a light repast. Every member is a Shanachie (story teller), though the topics are diverse. Since our heritage is both North and South, we do not touch upon "the throubles" of that sainted land.

I belong to the Burleigh Glee Club, five guys who meet once a year on a secluded island on Stoney Lake. The cottage is Victorian and charming. To be honest we do not sing, but discuss politics and settle the affairs of the nation. As a result, democracy continues to flourish.

On the second Tuesday of the month I play poker with a bunch of cutthroats. Well, not really. It is just penny ante, with lots of talk and plenty of laughter. Last week I lost three bucks. Was someone dealing from the bottom of the deck?

Then there are the guys I meet for lunch. We swap tall tales and reminisce. Sometimes we touch on the serious, but usually we just enjoy.

But back to the four immortals:

The first is a chap that I walked to school with all the days of my youth. He was not of my religious persuasion, but we managed to hopscotch the issue. Frequently on a soft autumn day, we would skip school and go partridge hunting. We often double-dated and told each other ridiculous lies. Now we only see one another several times a year, but if I need him, Bill Jones is just a telephone call away.

Another friend is a surgeon, Bill Blastorah, a creature of mercurial temperament, quick to anger, a tad short of total belligerence. We relish argumentative talks. It is only my soft voice and gentle sway that circumvent total mayhem. Since he has operated on me a couple of times, he knows me inside and out, the quality of myself, and this keeps him at bay.

One day, some time ago, there was a knock at my back door. Who should be standing there but Jimmy Monaghan, a friend I had not seen in 30 years who had emigrated to the United States. He was wearing a Tilley hat and carrying a large duffle bag. Over a highball, he told me of a shattered romance and a recent colostomy. I told him of my own experience with colon surgery. As members of the cancer fraternity, we clinked glasses. We had beaten the devils, at least for a time. Six months later, Jim's body was discovered on his sailboat off the coast of Malibu. Requiescat in pace, old buddy!

Three hundred years ago a man said, and I quote: "Old friends are best. King James II used to call for his old shoes, they were easiest on his feet."

I have saved my very best friend for the conclusion. On a certain St. Valentine's day a thousand moons ago, I married her. She also is not of my religious persuasion. Why do I get mixed up with these people? But when I hurt, she winces. When I laugh, she smiles. When I despair, she promises a better tomorrow, and she is generally right. Please don't tell her I said so; she could get carried away. In truth, I think I'll tell her myself, and bear the consequences. You see she is even closer than the telephone.

The girl that I married.

"Of all the means to ensure happiness throughout the whole of life, by far the most important is the acquisition of friends." (Epicurus).

Echoes Of A Bygone Christmas

Every year about this time, I take a walking tour of our downtown. I wait till near dusk to experience that special twilight atmosphere.

I spent half a century on this thoroughfare, this George Street, making a livelihood, sometimes merely an existence. This year I am confining my attention to that portion of George Street just south of Simcoe.

I light a cigarette, lean against a lamp standard, slit my eyes -and the years roll backwards.

Across the way are: McDermid's Drugs, Patterson Surplus, Kent Shoes, The Sally Shoppe, Selkirk's Men's Wear (since I was in this business, I secretly envied their patronage - always busier than a barefoot cat on a hot tin roof).

Over there: Reitman's Ladies Wear, Tamblyn Drugs, Comstock Furniture, the Laura Secord Shop, the Robert Simpson Order Office, Barrie Furs, the Capital Theatre, CN Telegraph office, Elsie Bennett Jewelry, The Deluxe Café.

I remember the Christmas trees lining the streets, not decorated, not lighted, just simple unadorned evergreens. I see three sisters of the Order of St. Joseph hustling along with their shopping bags. They are all talking at once; they are excited. I spot the pastor of St. Peter's Cathedral, then, here comes the rector of George Street United Church. Does the liturgical calendar influence shopping habits? Perhaps so.

Groups of young carollers perform outside the brightly decorated shop windows. They are collecting funds for Christmas hampers. Over there on the corner, a Santa Claus is ringing his bell. His costume is four sizes too large for him.

Because it is Saturday, Eaton's will shroud their display windows with full-length drapes at closing time, for despite the Yuletide season, Mr. Eaton does not believe in commercialism on the sabbath.

Down the street comes a snowplough, not a machine engineered by Bombardier, but a Clydesdale horse with arched neck and feathered fetlocks, bells ajingle, dragging a wooden plough, wedge-shaped, with the driver walking within the V, holding loose reins. Pedestrians immediately give way, for there is something mighty intimidating about a full-grown Clyde, despite the feathered fetlocks. It is a welcome sight, but the snow piles up along the curbside to a height of almost five feet.

The streets are thronged with people, old people, young people, babies in sleighs with parcels tucked around them, everyone calling "Merry Christmas"; and over there on the corner of Simcoe Street, the Salvation Army Band is playing, reminding us of that very special "Silent Night, Holy Night".

I spot a couple of our local gambling fraternity cruising down the street, both niftily dressed. I wonder where the crap game is tonight.

A chap I know leaves a popular hotel, brushes rudely by me. He has obviously been over-served. When he gets home the missus will tear a strip off him. Too much of the Christmas spirit!

And what will be under the tree on Christmas morning? Slippers, gloves, mittens, pajamas. My sisters will get velvet galoshes trimmed with fur. The boys will receive galoshes as well, but they will have snap buckle closures. Or just maybe aviator boots, the kind that are never fastened, but left open, as if you had just climbed out of the cockpit of a Spitfire.

If you are cold, you can step inside any of the shops and get warm. They'll even let you leave your packages so you won't have to lug them around all evening while you are shopping.

The Christmas chimes at St. John's Anglican Church are ringing out. It is time to go. And besides, a young police officer across the street is viewing me with suspicion. Well, why not? Some guy, leaning against a lamp post with slitted eyes is naturally suspect. To put him at ease, I call out: "Merry Christmas, Constable". He smiles and waves back. I guess I wasn't a serious suspect.

It is getting late. The chatelaine and Bonnie Bluebell will be concerned, probably walking down the road to meet me.

I enter the house. Not a stir. I open the bedroom door, and there they are, the two gals in my life, fast asleep. I close the door gently not to disturb. I pour myself a coffee, liberally laced with Amaretto. And why not? For me it has been an emotional day.

I carry my coffee to the window and glance up into the sky, like the shepherds and the wise men did 2000 years go. I see nothing. But I am not disillusioned. As an editor of The New York Sun said in 1897: *"Oh, yes, Virginia, there is a Santa Claus. Your friends are wrong. They have been affected by the scepticism of a sceptical age. He exists as certainly as love, generosity and devotion exist."*

I think I will light the fire, awaken the girls, put on a couple of Christmas tapes. Tonight I am going to make hamburgers, better than Wendy himself - and we will have a grand time.

Tomorrow night I will check the sky again, looking for that special star. And by the way, before my mind flits away: MERRY CHRISTMAS, EVERYONE!

Bonnie Bluebell dreams of Santa.

It is my father himself I see reflected.

The New Year - Maturity And Retirement

As the New Year makes its stealthy entrance, it seems time to examine one's lifestyle, aspirations and even maturity.

Random House defines maturity as full development, perfected condition - or overripe. I subscribe to the latter. It took me considerable time to reach this condition, but like the chrysanthemum, I am a late bloomer.

I arise in the morning, insert my denture and assemble the other parts. I emerge from the shower and examine my mirrored image. It is my father himself I see reflected - the same spare figure, white hair and deeply etched face.

I miss my walks in the woods, but concern has been expressed that I might stumble and fall, and it would take the authorities 28 days to locate my remains. Remains are important; otherwise you can't have a proper "wake". I can see it now. Perhaps his excellency the bishop will do a walk-on, with the Knights of Columbus providing an honour guard. Both are unlikely, but hopes that spring eternal distinguish us from the beasts of the field.

Frequently on my way to Mass, I will stop at the cemetery and visit some of the family graves. There is my grandmother, an austere lady. Across the road on the rise, and well apart, is the resting place of my great-grandfather, Garrett Galvin. I was told he was a private person, which might account for the reclusive grave-site.

I am beginning to sound morbid. In reality, I kick in a pretty good time. I read a lot - newspapers, journals and re-read Dickens, Yeats, a few others. I meet with old friends twice a week for lunch and story-telling. Some of the stories are repeated over and over again. What does it matter? It's kinda fun to know the punchline in advance.

Of course there are some problems. I go down stairs clutching the bannister with more fervour than I would expend on a vestal virgin in the days of my youth. (The vestals all lived in the north end - did you know that?)

The house has a thousand secrets, and the chatelaine knows them all. If the television isn't functioning properly, you just kick the lower right hand corner and the problem is solved. The other day, one of the elements on the stove wasn't working. I reported this to the chatelaine, and her response was: "Change your shoes." Not to question her wisdom, I did as she directed. When nothing happened, I complained to the chatelaine and showed her my change of footwear. She put a gentle hand on my shoulder, and in a more audible voice said: "Fuse. Change the fuse, not your shoes." Life continues to be a learning experience.

I pick up the portable telephone and try to change the television channel. It doesn't work. Bell Canada ought to do something about this. To cut down on my smoking, I hide my cigarette lighter, then I can't find it and I experience withdrawal. I drive my car with great care and reduced speed, sometimes to the impatience of a following motorist. I use my flasher to indicate a turn, and in addition extend my arm out the window in the old way to doubly safeguard. I can say with pride that I have never had an accident, but I have probably caused several.

I keep irregular hours, sometimes arising at 4 a.m. to putter about, or sleeping till noon. Right now the clock reads 6:30 a.m., and in the east, dawn appears to be shrugging itself awake. I must make some moves. Last night's dinner dishes to do, the kitchen floor needs scrubbing, and the livingroom should be vacuumed. As I previously reported, I do all the household chores - the chatelaine has become more or less a toy, albeit a pleasant creature, very neat about her person.

But first, on such a promising day I will take Bonnie Bluebell for a walk. She will enjoy that. B.B. flatly refuses to move. Sometimes it can be a lonely old town. This day I will put on a suit and a proper shirt and tie (looking like one of the 12), and do my weekly tour of downtown to reassure myself that the merchants and the City council have a proper handle on things.

"Dawn appears to be shrugging itself awake."

Some day you, too, will enjoy the experience of retirement - and (God willing) maturity. By the way, regarding my aspirations for '97, I don't think I will change one thing.

Escaping The Winter Blahs

To escape the winter blahs and the March lion, the chatelaine and himself drove south. Our destination - Destin itself - is located on the panhandle of the State of Florida. Now, a mini city, I can remember when it was a tiny fishing village. It is naturally not as tropical as more southerly places, but the price of admission appeals to my miserly soul.

Several months ago, Hurricane Opal swept through this coastal area with appalling results. Entire buildings were demolished. If you saw a structure with an entire roof, it was either a Roman Catholic church or the National Guard Armoury - both enterprises being involved with self-discipline.

Now, the chatelaine does all the long-distance driving because I suffer from vertigo; even broad vistas give me the trembles. I understand St. Thomas Aquinas experienced this affliction, so no apologies. As for my role in the endeavour, I handle the tape deck, playing music of the '50s, and hand-feed Elizabeth ju jubes. Gasoline is not cheap, but on a long automobile trip those jubes can run into a bundle.

As we approached the Ambassador Bridge in Detroit, to indulge my phobia, I retired to the rear seat of the car, threw a tartan blanket over my head and repeated my mantra. When we reached American immigration, the chatelaine handed over our passports. The uniformed official enquired: "What's that in the back seat?" Her response: "My husband."

The official said: "He's going to have to remove the blanket so I can have a gander at him." I did not know, but according to American law, one cannot enter the United States with a blanket over one's head.

One morning, as was our habit, we pulled into a station to gas up. It was self service. I started the pump and then went to the kiosk to buy some chocolate bars. Thinking the operation complete, Elizabeth drove away from the tank with the hose still attached to the car. The spillage cost me an extra $15 and angry words and looks from an employee who immediately hosed down the area so Atlanta would not burn again.

Farther south in Alabama, we once more left the interstate to refuel. The station was a shack. Sitting on a bench in front were four rough-looking chappies. One had a long rifle on his lap. I was reminded of the movie *"Deliverance"*. They examined me with too much interest. I wanted to get the hell out of there, but the proprietor appeared, sporting a six-day growth of beard, with a nail penetrating the waistband of his trousers, and gripping one suspender. I requested $5 worth of gas. He replied: "Well, while I'm here, I might as well fill it up." My response was: "Splendid."

Then he said: "Those wipers of yours don't look good. Better have a new set." I readily agreed, and added: "Splendid."

Once again on Route 65, I commented to the chatelaine: "These rednecks attempt to intimidate a person. I won't buy that action." She said: "Relax, Clare. My window was down; I heard everything. I think you behaved splendidly."

Destin shoulders Fort Elgin air base, the largest in the world. The last time we visited this area, the Gulf War was in progress and the skies were filled with military aircraft. Not this time.

After four nights on the road, we arrived at our condo with the blue and emerald coastal view. In renting this accommodation, I had emphatically stipulated: "Nothing above the third floor." We were lodged on the seventh floor. I left the elevator and actually crawled on my hands and knees down the open corridor to our unit. Three of the walls of our apartment were totally mirrored. The place resembled a Venetian bawdy house (not that I ever attended one, but I read a lot). The dishwasher leaked and the microwave didn't work. I can endure most hardships providing the microwave works. However, the view from the balcony was spectacular and occasionally, after a martini, I would venture through the sliding doors.

We could see, just a few hundred yards away, a new beach house, large, imposing grey brick with a dune walk to the gulf. We were told that this was owned by the author John Grisham. We kept an eagle eye on the place, but never did get to see the great writer.

On our way home, we were six days and five nights on the road. Within 170 miles of Peterborough, because of fog and torrential rain, we were forced to get off the highway and seek accommodation. The motel we found was interesting. I believe it was once used as the outbuilding of a detention centre. Even the TV was unique. The audio did not match the video. I picked up an old re-run. Olivier was gazing at the beautiful oval face of Merle Oberon. Grasping her by the shoulders, he asked: "When did you last visit Wendy's?"

In the adjoining unit four men were playing 7-card stud. It was not a serious game. There were sounds of revelry and the clink of bottles, and Harry never should have attempted to fill in that straight, but that is the hope that lies eternal in the heart of every bad poker player. The last thing I remember before I drifted off was Harry saying: "I'll see you, and raise you a buck."

Well, we finally made it home to "the holy land". That night I had a dream and Aquinas spoke to me: "You idiot! Why didn't you catch a flight? I always do!" You see, people with my affliction can fly in comfort, so long as they are totally disconnected with the earth they do not experience vertigo.

All in all I would recommend Destin. Forget Miami! Down there they shoot horses. And you will love the Gulf of Mexico. After a martini you can catch a peek at the splendour through the sliding doors.

Barefoot on the beach at Destin, Florida.

The cottage on Chemong Lake. – 1950 –

Fishing With Dad

The snow is melting; broad patches of lawn are appearing; robins are tramping across the soggy ground, and soon the ice will be gone, the pickerel season will open - and I will go fishing.

It seems, and even worse, feels like a century ago that I would go fishing with my father. He was a man of medium frame with a shock of white hair and the bluest eyes in the diocese. He was a good Christian, practising his religion, but never wearing it like a banner on his sleeve. My father acquired a red, pointed-end punt, and he would sit on the prow and paddle forever. It bothered me because my dad could not swim. This seemed strange to me, but then, most of our aboriginal neighbours at Curve Lake, who spent so much time on the waterways also lacked this accomplishment.

Our heavy trolling lines were wrapped around a birch block, and our lures were large silver Buffalo spoons. I can close my eyes and see the spoons flashing in the darkened waters. We would fish the skirts of the Chemong Lake floating bridge (the longest in the world) and watch the automobiles passing each other on the pull-outs with the water halfway up the hubcaps. I felt safer in the punt - crossing the bridge twice a day solved any bowel obstruction.

Fishing was a sporting venture, but the catch also supplemented our Friday diet, the day when Micks were not supposed to eat meat. We no longer adhere to this custom; at least I don't.

My father worked hard and earned a modest living. He was a quiet man who kept his own counsel, but lent an ear to anyone who came to him with a problem. I don't wish to portray him as a saint, but he was someone to emulate - and sometimes I did, but only occasionally, to my chagrin.

On these fishing excursions, as my father sat puffing contentedly on his pipe, I chattered away. Talk, talk, talk, talk. Then I would catch him observing me, the thought in his head: "Did I really sire this metronome?" I regained his approval when I felt a tug on my line and, hand over hand, boated a large-mouth bass.

Sometimes, if the lake was calm, we would extend our trip and pass the old cemetery on the lake, the spot where my forebears landed as Irish famine immigrants, one hundred and seventy years ago: Garrett, 50 years of age, with his family, including one of his children - six-year-old Patrick, my great-grandfather. Dad would make the sign of the cross, and I would follow suit.

Then it was time to drop anchor and have our lunch of homemade bread and thick bologna sandwiches, with a thermos of hot tea. The Savoy in London could not provide anything more delicious.

Suddenly my father's birch block starts to chatter. He's caught a lunge, and a big one. I'm excited. I do an Arapaho fertility dance. My dad says: "Sit down, boy. You're rocking the boat." I do. Fifteen minutes later we capture the creature. It's a beaut. Friday's dinner.

When we arrived back at the cottage, Mother would be waiting on the dock, concerned about our long absence. Later she'd query me: "Did you enjoy your day with your father? Did you talk his leg off?" When I answered in the affirmative, she would say: "Well that's good. With your chatter and all that fresh air, he'll sleep soundly tonight."

This spring I will repeat those fishing trips, with my brand new spinning rod approved by the outdoor writers. It won't be the same though, without the man sitting on the point with his endless paddling and pipe smoking. I can't crank back the years, but I can close my eyes and go back in memory. He's right there on the prow, and I am chattering away, and the Buffalo spoons are flashing in the black waters.

And I am young - about one hundred years ago.

The dock.

Once I Had A Friend Called Sarah

Once upon a time when I was young, about table-high, a tad closer to the turn of the last century than to the one forthcoming, I had a friend called Sarah. She occupied a second-floor apartment immediately next door to the house where I was conceived and raised. Sarah was one of the homeliest women that I have ever encountered: tall, angular, grey thinning hair, prominent dentures with a large mole on the bridge of her nose sprouting a tiny hair. She was about 100 years old, but then remember I was only table-high, and anyone over 60 seemed to me to be nudging the century mark.

Sorry, I forgot to tell you that Sarah Collins was one of the nicest women I ever met, and my good friend. I would tap on her front door and enquire, "Like a little company?" And I was always welcome. She would make toast in a wire clamp device, stove top, and slather the result with butter and orange jam, and then as a treat, we would wash it down with green tea. Gawd, I haven't had green tea in years.

Despite my youth I was always treated as a contemporary and Sarah was truly interested in the life and times of myself. Her prayer book and daily missal were only a palm away. Often she would read a chapter and we would discuss the philosophy - not always agreeing. (If you think Sarah was a religious nut, you are wrong. Years later I thought she must have been an agnostic). The chapter readings were meant to be provocative, open for discussion.

I had no idea of her source of income, but her clothing was obviously expensive, and she often wore suede gloves. She had been born in Dublin she told me, and her fiance had been killed at the Battle of Ypres in the First Great War. He had been a real charmer, she said, and looked just like John Barrymore, with the integrity of Ronald Coleman. No wonder she loved him. She wore a large signet ring on her forefinger, and I assumed it once belonged to the hero of Ypres.

Sorry again. I forgot to tell you that Sarah taught me to play Parcheesi (a form of backgammon) and the competitive spirit ran high. Sometimes when it rained, we would go out on the covered balcony and watch the deluge and ponder the mysteries of life. I suppose that as a lad I should have been playing scrub football across the street in the Albion field, but to trade that for an afternoon with Sarah? Not on your life. I recall the time she told me that one day I would be famous: a lawyer, a doctor, an Indian chief. Since the two forerunners were quite beyond me, I wondered how a youngster of Irish Catholic origin could qualify for Native status.

There was a childless widower just up the street who admired Sarah, and he would bring her produce from his garden. Though she appreciated his kindness, the man and his gifts were poor substitutes for a genuine hero. She was, however, quick to admit that the parsnips fried in butter were really quite tasty.

She would regale me with stories of Ireland - the poverty, the English oppression, the secret Irish societies; while I sat captivated, white-knuckling the footstool at her side.

There was a distinctive odour about Sarah, nothing objectionable, because she was always immaculate, but there was a suggestion of camphor, as if she had been hanging in a closet too long.

One summer I spent three weeks with my paternal grandmother. This was not kegs of fun, but an obligation imposed by my father. On my return home, I hugged my mother and then raced over to see Sarah. (Do you remember when you were a kid, you never walked anywhere, you raced to wherever you were going, because the days were too short?)

There was no response when I pounded on her door. I couldn't understand this. She was always there. When I returned home, Mother informed me that Sarah had moved. "Where?" I asked. She didn't know because Miss Collins was a very private person. How could she have gone away without telling me?

I lost track of Sarah. Some six years later, I read her obituary in the newspaper. I went to the funeral home to attend her wake, and I asked the funeral director to please put on Sarah's glasses; she just didn't look right without them. The service was poorly attended. I suppose this was understandable; she had kept to herself so much, but the widower up the street with the cabbages and the parsnips was there.

I found out that Sarah had lied to me. She hadn't been born in Dublin at all, but was raised six miles east of our town limits. And there had been no boyfriend. But it was okay. I, myself, have been known to tell the odd fib.

I missed Sarah Collins. Next to my mother, she had become the most important woman in my young life.

I still think of her sometimes. Tomorrow, I am going to go shopping - buy some orange jam and green tea. It's been years since I have had a real treat. And perhaps I can coerce the chatelaine into a game of Parcheesi.

A Brush With The Fuzz

I have never been charged under the Criminal Code, or for that matter, the Highway Traffic Act. When I was in business, I fitted the local police and the OPP officers of No. 8 District with uniforms. So I did have the occasional brush with the constabulary.

One evening about the witching hour, I was returning to my home. As I was passing Montgomery's swamp just south of the Bridgenorth Pines Pavilion, I was overtaken by an OPP cruiser. The officer advised me that my tail light was malfunctioning. I assured him on my honour that tomorrow it would be corrected.

He then queried: "Are you subject to seizures?" I answered in the negative. He told me that he had been following me for some time and that I appeared to be gesturing wildly.

My reply: "No problem, Constable; you see I had the radio on and I was conducting the New York Philharmonic." And I added: "You should see me in action with the Boston Pops."

He turned, then returned. "Look, do me a favour. I'm due to be transferred the end of the month. Until then, would you please stay away from the New York Philharmonic and totally avoid the Boston Pops?"

Before he left the diocese, he stopped me once again, about the same hour and location. At the time I was driving a borrowed car, and suddenly a voice out of nowhere said: "Sir, you are low in petrol." I hit one ditch, then the opposite ditch and finally corrected. Then the fuzz appeared. Same guy.

"You weren't into the Boston Pops again?"

"No, Sir. I am sticking to Gregorian chants." Then I told him about the strange voice.

"Get rid of this vehicle," he advised. "I don't think you can handle it emotionally."

One early morning as I was hustling into town late for a dental appointment, I noticed a plain car in the rear vision mirror. Moments later a red flashing light appeared on its roof and I was overtaken. "Your licence, please:" the officer demanded. "You were speeding."

I explained about the late dental appointment, my previous chaste character, the fact that my aunt was terminally ill. Making no impression, I told him I was a Roman Catholic. He released me on my own recognizance with the comment: "On your way. Slow down. And remember, you owe a Methodist a favour." I never understood those people.

Another morning at exactly 10:15 a.m., I received a telephone call from an inspector of the local force. (I always check my watch in the event a terrorist bomb has exploded in Norwood - so I will know the exact time.) I was told to appear in his office in 10 minutes. Click went the phone. I was indignant, but I did as I was told.

His opener: "Where were you last night between the hours of 11 p.m. and 2 a.m.?" I couldn't remember, so I lied. "I was at home in my jams watching reruns of the Simpson Family."

He opened his desk drawer, checked a TV Guide and said: "You lie."

"Who me?"

Truth itself can be chancy. If your wife asks: "How do you like my new hairdo?" and you tell her the truth, it could be a long winter.

Then the inspector handed me a VISA credit card, my VISA credit card. "This card was found at the scene of a break-in last night in the west end."

Indeed. The chatelaine had carelessly left the card in the glove compartment and failed to lock the car. I was furious with the entire world. As I rose to leave, the constable behind me drew his revolver and the inspector said: "You don't leave until you have been mugged and fingerprinted. Take him downstairs."

I am easily intimidated. My attack dog intimidates me, and she only weighs five pounds. I preceded the constable, brushing shoulders with some of the uniforms in the corridor.

On the way back to my shop, I sat on a bench in Victoria Park and reviewed my criminal record. Those uniforms didn't fit that badly. Then it suddenly dawned on me. I had been HAD. It was a scam! A whiz! A joke! I wiped my damp hands with a Kleenex.

In conclusion: There ought to be a society for the prevention of cruelty to poor unfortunate Catholics.

The Railroad Station

Railroad lines throughout our fair nation are being closed down, the steel torn up; what remains the government is trying to privatize. Do you remember when you were a kid, how you would wave to the engineer when a train went by, and he would wave back? Do you remember that feeling of excitement when you heard the train whistle and the "whoosh" of the steam exhaust as the engine came to a halt?

A dozen platform scenes flash across my mind: A newly-wed couple embarking on their honeymoon, surrounded by the wedding party who throw sufficient rice to support a Cantonese family for a month. The honeymoon destination, Buffalo, or some other exotic place. The bustle of arrival and departure at Christmas and Easter time, not commuters, but people coming home or leaving on a holiday. The conductor's final "All Aboard!" as he swings up the steps of the passenger car. The finality and the hush as the train pulls out of sight.

I remember saying goodbye to my brother Fabian at the CPR station. He was a chronic asthmatic, and his doctor had recommended Arizona's climate. We hugged emotionally, and he was gone. I would not see his face for five years. Fabian, an accomplished skier, never got beyond Banff and there he stayed.

I barely remember my maternal aunt and uncle arriving from Saskatchewan with their children, all standing in a line on the station's platform. The dust storms had blown their homestead and dreams away. They stayed with us until they were re-established. There were happy times, and there were glimpses of sadness. Once I remember seeing a trainman unloading a rough box onto the luggage cart, with a mortician and a hearse waiting nearby; someone wanting to be buried in their home parish.

I remember seeing the long flat cars transporting canons and searchlights made by our CGE plant, bound for some European war zone. And still longer ago, I remember the heartbreak of the '30s and the hoboes riding the rails, leaving home, trying to find employment, trying to survive.

There was a period in my young life when I was keeping company with an attractive nurse in Toronto. Saturday nights I would catch the 6 p.m. to the "Big Smoke". On boarding, I always headed for the chair and dining car where I would join a local hotel proprietor at his table. This gentleman attended more hockey games than Foster Hewitt himself. His opening line was always: "It's a cold evening, Clare, but fortunately...". At this point he would open his valise and produce a jar, and the coolish atmosphere would be dispelled.

It seemed that the best food was served on trains. The waiter, in his starched tunic and black tie, would take our order and make suggestions. Still later the chef would appear to ensure that everything was satisfactory. As we lingered over a second cup of tea, the train pulled into Union Station.

On one occasion I was in Hamilton on a business trip. At lunch time I took a walk down Cannon Street. In front of me was a tow-headed youngster on a tricycle. Suddenly he fell over on the turf and was sick to his stomach. I was able to determine where he lived, and with the child under one arm and his bike under the other, I found the modest dwelling in the rear of an auto body shop. It was not the kind of place that would be included in an annual tour of homes. I neglected to tell you that the morning Globe (read on board the train) had reported an outbreak of polio in the Hamilton area.

At 1:00 a.m. the conductor shook me awake: "You are home, Clare!" I stood up and fell flat on my face. "What's wrong with you?" the conductor asked. "My god, I've got polio!", I yelled.

The understanding man then suggested that my leg was asleep. "Put your arm over my shoulder, and we will take a little walk." It worked. If you ever contract polio, travel CPR and take a walk with the conductor. Just maybe a miracle will happen.

Jack Ainslie told me about a train in Newfoundland that stopped so the passengers could get out and pick blueberries. Those were the days, my friend!

It appears that the era of the Iron Horse is coming to a close. I am certain that the trans-Canada run will continue, but it won't be stopping at places such as Peterborough or Lakefield. So, if you harbour a penchant for waving at railroad engineers, you will have to go elsewhere.

As for me, I'm seriously considering an excursion on the Orient Express.

My Guest, The Ghost

In my journeys to the past which are flavoured with a hint of fantasy, by and large I maintain a firm grip on reality, thanks to the evening prayers of my two sisters and the parish priest.

I study the writings and seek the counsel of Francis Hinks Dobbin, born 1850, associated with the Peterborough Daily Review, and local historian emeritus. He is due to arrive!

This fall day, the prospect from my window is depressing, the incessant rain and wind have harvested the leaves and robbed me of a tapestry of colour. I hear a rustle, turn and there he is: Francis Dobbin, seated in the Cogswell chair, ramrod straight, his hair neatly combed, moustache trimmed with care, his suit and cravat of Edwardian fashion, his neat boots laced and ankle high. One hand cradles an unlit pipe.

Our salutations are brief because we both have things to do and places to go. His opener: "Weather got you down, Clare? Not to worry; soon winter will be upon us and the autumn debris will be cloaked in ermine." It is common knowledge that people of his era functioned with a modest vocabulary, lacking expletives such as neat, cool, awesome, ballistic.

My ghostly apparition continues: "Did I ever tell you about Peterborough's greatest snowstorm. The year was 1870. It began on March 13, and continued for six days and nights. Downtown merchants were kept busy shovelling the six-foot plank sidewalks, to no avail. The situation worsened. With the waist high snow, no one could go to work and school children were kept at home. No funerals could be held, and the police force, though ever vigilant, made no arrests. Our 14 saloons enjoyed scant patronage hawking whisky at 25 cents a gallon (I would have taken up permanent residence). A red marker placed on a door signified the occupants were low in victuals. Could you help?

Communication with the outside world was by telegraph only and seven trains were hung up between Toronto and our town. Three teams of oxen, with improvised snowploughs, were deployed. The creatures could make no progress. At the corner of George and Simcoe Streets, the snow was 11 feet high.

"Then came Spring, blessed Spring, with a thaw and wild flooding. Dams along the Otonabee River gave way and there was tremendous damage. For the French-Canadian river log runners, it meant terror. Our Little Lake overflowed and water, 16 inches deep, flowed down Lock Street. Lands later occupied by the Canadian General Electric and the Canadian Pacific Railway were inundated. Our gentle, sweet flowing Otonabee became a tyrant. Funeral entourages to Little Lake Cemetery were transported by punt and skiff."

My enthralled attention is distracted by two things happening in chorus. There is a prolonged rustling and when I turn, my ghostly guest has disappeared, the aroma of his pipe tobacco lingering in the air (an English cut, I believe). Suddenly the side door is rudely thrust open. Enter the chatelaine.

Excitedly, I tell her of my visitor, but she is forever the sceptic. I don't wish this to be widely known, but she does not embrace my religious persuasion, which would account for her irresponsibility. None-the-less, Mr. Dobbin will return. We have much to offer one another, though he has a lot of catching up to do. He will regale me with local past history, and I will instruct him in current vocabulary such as: COOL, NEAT, AWESOME and BALLISTIC.

A fair exchange. Would you not say so yourself?

Francis Hinks Dobbin

A Day Like Any Other Day

As my reader is aware (I hear it's all over town), since my retirement, I have assumed all household chores, the cleaning and the cooking - the chatelaine merely a toy. With respect to my cooking: I know that by even lifting the telephone would gain me a permanent berth at the Royal York. My fame has spread; Good Housekeeping is featuring "Himself" in the March edition.

The time is 6 a.m. I feel a pressure on my chest. My family is prone to heart irregularities. I whisper a prayer for the dying. The pressure moves. I snap on the bedside lamp and gaze into the black eyes of Bonnie Bluebell, my little dog. She wants to "go bathrooms" outside. I shrug into a disreputable hooded terry robe. I catch a reflection of myself in the dresser mirror. I resemble an ancient Druid.

It is raining - not gentle rain, but a deluge. Bonnie Bluebell seizes the opportunity to inspect the entire foundation of our premises. I could kill her. We re-enter the house and I towel her down. Moments later there is a complaint from the opposite court: "Bonnie is soaking wet. Did you towel her?" My response: "I did!" A further muffled query: "Did you use the blow dryer?" I confessed my failure. In my advanced years, and state of health, blow-drying a dog at 6 a.m. does not exactly light up my board. Undoubtedly I am irresponsible.

It is too late to return to my sleeping bag. I plan breakfast: juice, a hot cereal, a small omelette, a muffin, Earl Grey tea. The reaction on presentation is mostly negative. "I'll settle for the muffin" is the comment. I curl my fists. The job at the Royal York becomes more enticing.

Then my fan club starts calling.

Irene: "My bath tub is plugged, and company is coming."

Himself: "Use baking soda and vinegar."

Penny: "Would you have the spice, saffron, in your cupboard?"

Himself: "I do and I have."

Penny aspires to becoming a talented cook. When her husband's body is discovered a coroner's inquest will be necessary.

Eileen: "Clare, dear, I'm attending the Casino and my washing machine just died. I need my slacks washed, and the hem on the right leg has come down."

Himself: "Bring them up. I'll look after it."

I leave the phone off the hook. I can't be all things to all people.

I enter the sun room. I am alarmed. The woman I pledged my troth to is performing elaborate gyrations, perhaps some involved Protestant religious ritual. She informs me she is practising Tai Chi. What the hell is that?

I wonder if there is a Valium in the house - and also, with the early morning exposure, I have a fever and a pain in my chest. With trembling hands, I prepare a Neo Citran.

I go grocery shopping. At the store I pick up a flyer listing the specials. I've forgotten my glasses. I've forgotten my list. I improvise. Bobbie and Shirley, the two cashiers, are busier than a team of one-armed paperhangers. Judging from the quantity of groceries heaped in the cart immediately in front of me, I think the customer must operate an orphanage. One kindly staff woman, realizing I am on the verge of a nervous breakdown, opens a third cashdrawer, passes me through and summons a stalwart lad to carry out my bags. I follow him, lurching significantly.

Then the housekeeping. I have a gut feeling that I am getting a brand new vacuum cleaner for Christmas. Ah, the hope that lies eternal in the breast of man.

My sister-in-law is coming for dinner. She lived on the Continent for some time, a gourmet who shows talent in her own kitchen. My God, I don't think I can handle it. An hour before her arrival, I slip over to the village and purchase a large pizza. At dinner's end, the sister compliments me.

"Excellent," she says, "you must give me your recipe." I'm sensitive enough to blush. Then over her left shoulder I receive a concealed wink. Our dinner guest is a good sort.

I retire early to bed, exhausted long before the witching hour. I am about to succumb, when I feel a weight on my chest - and the black eyes are staring at me. Again I fumble for the Druid robe.

UNCLE JOE - and the Junior Ranger

My mother, Catherine Reid, was born in Kinmount, Ont. She had two sisters, Anne and Mary, plus a baby brother, Joseph. In the space of a year, both parents died, one with heart disease, the other with dropsy. The children were sent to different foster homes and tenuous contact was kept.

Prior to World War I, Joseph emigrated to the United states, eventually joining the Texas Rangers and going overseas as a member of the military police. On his return, correspondence with my mother was brisk, then slow, then non-existent.

The years trailed by, until one day my mother received a letter from a deputy sheriff in North Dakota. He wrote of a man he had befriended who lived in a local rooming house. This man had obviously had police experience, but was now suffering from amnesia. In an effort to help him, the deputy had searched his luggage and found in a side pocket of one of the bags a crumpled envelope bearing a name and address (my mother's). A detailed description of the amnesiac was included in the letter. Could he be a family member?

My mother immediately telephoned the deputy. It was her brother Joseph. She would come and get him. The response was: "No, ma'am. His health is robust, his mind is alert, except for loss of memory. But he is fiercely independent. He will come under his own power."

I sat on the verandah every afternoon awaiting the Texas Ranger. In my mind's eye, I could see him: double-breasted tan shirt, whipcord trousers, open road hat, .45 calibre Colt Peacemaker swinging at his hip - and the shining star, his badge.

One day I was rewarded and equally disappointed. A brand new 1932 Ford Cabriolet with Dakota plates pulled up in front of our house. Out stepped a very tall man wearing a dark grey, three-piece suit, white shirt and maroon tie. True, his boots were cowboy style, but is this what a Texas Ranger looks like? Then it dawned - he's working undercover! The nuns had taught me everything.

It was interesting watching the brother and sister together. A shyness, a nervousness, an apprehension, then suddenly a close embrace and the years fell away. None of the neighbours were invited in to share the reunion. Mom wanted to keep Uncle Joe for herself, alone.

It was a time for celebration. We went on picnics together to historic places, such as Omemee and Ennismore. Then, one significant day - to Kinmount. We had lunch on the Reid Road where the siblings were born, the road having been named for their family. The atmosphere was a tad subdued. On that particular occasion, I learned a bit of my family heritage. My grandmother was a McGee. Directly related to Thomas D'Arcy McGee, brilliant Irish-Canadian poet, journalist, orator and politician, Father of Confederation and the victim of Canada's first political assassination. Wow! Mother encouraged me to try to emulate this man. In the first instance, it was quite beyond me, and secondly, it was too late. Also, the prospect of being shot in the back by some political nut was not a thigh-slapping prospect. But I remembered the connection!

One time, when my mother was picking wild flowers, Uncle Joe swore me in as a Junior Texas Ranger. That summer I became a tyrant. I arrested seven neighbours. They were all released for lack of evidence. It became a mark of neighbourhood distinction to be collared by the Junior Ranger. My law enforcement career was hampered by Mother's edict: I had to be home by dark, even though any self-respecting sleuth knows that most crimes are committed on the stroke of midnight, damn it.

One evening after supper, Uncle Joe gave me a sealed envelope and instructed: "Open this when you are alone." I did. Inside the envelope was a German Iron Cross decoration. I sat on the edge of the bed sweating light bulbs. Ranger Joe Reid - a traitor! My God, if that came to light he would be hanged for treason. Mr. Roosevelt himself would spring the trap. After a near sleepless night, I cornered Mother in the pantry. I started, but she interrupted. "Oh! So it's about the Iron Cross. Well, that was given to him by a German prisoner-of-war who was very ill and later died. Joe showed him some kindness, and the man gave it to Joe in appreciation, a token of esteem. It was significant to Joe. That's why he wanted you to have it." Now, how could I have entertained such thoughts about my uncle - and the two of us Texas Rangers?

Well, Uncle Joe returned to the Sates, and was employed as head of security by a wealthy upper state New York banking magnate. A few years later, he married an American woman. They visited us on several occasions.

When the second world conflict became imminent, I tried to enlist in military intelligence. The burly recruit sergeant appreciated my Ranger background and informed me that normally they did not accept anyone as short as I was. However, in his wisdom he decreed that I was "in" but "underground". The orders were that I was to report back every six months. And only to him. His closing comments: "For heaven's sake, Lad, be careful!" So instead of taking the wide paved thoroughfare to my home, I returned along the banks and bushes of Jackson Park Creek, sometimes obliterating my footprints. You never know when someone is following you.

Well, the days of being a Ranger attached to military intelligence are far behind me, but my life is anything but humdrum what with the likes of the chatelaine and my dog, Bonnie Bluebell, constantly in attendance, constantly a source of amazement.

My uncle, Joe Reid.

courtesy of Joyce Parnell

Saturday night at the Aragon - 1952. From left: Agnes Strickland, Bruce Upper, Don Earle, Barbara Hughes, Joyce Dewart, Garth Parnell.

The First Nightclub In Our Town

"*It was many and many a year ago, in a kingdom by the sea.*" To be honest, it was not a kingdom, but our town, and it was not the sea, but the Otonabee River. The time: about half a century ago. I was working at Dunn's Tailors eking out a modest living but filled with great expectations.

It was midmorning; suddenly the shop door was thrust open and in walked one Jack Wineberg, an acquaintance. He had rolls of parchment under his arm and the balance thrust into the loose waistband of his gallused trousers. He spread the papers on the cutting table. He had a dream - a nightclub.

Initially I was dubious. Didn't we already have the Brock Street Arena for dancing and entertainment? Then again, despite its modest tinsel and scanty decorations, it was still a hockey rink and halfway into a waltz you could run into a net. I got caught up with Wineberg's dream. He had an option on Lansdowne Street East property. McGinness Trailers were constructing a plant across the road; the City was prepared to run a water-line. The new club could hook in. Jack was looking for a building contractor. I suggest-ed Kell Sheehy; his office was in the old Cluxton building, a drop-kick away.

The resultant structure resembled an aircraft hangar, but building materials were in short supply. You did what you could; amenities would be added down the road - and they were.

I was present at the opening of Club Aragon. The famed orchestra of Ellis McClintock had been booked for the occasion, and one could feel the excitement that first night. It was *"just forty-five minutes from Broadway"*.

The premises boasted no liquor licence. You brought your own jug and stuffed it under the table. Splits (mix) could be purchased. The police would sometimes drop around, but it was cursory, unless the behaviour was bizarre. The resident orchestra was Bobbie Kinsman and his Band, with Orville Wainman, the male vocalist, and female singers Vi Wall and Nicki Humphries; Streak Konkle on base and Paul Minicola with his soft sax. Sometimes, if the fit was upon him, Buzz Buzzell would play *Sugar Blues*. Then the action would cease, everyone stood still and listened to the magic of Buzzell's trumpet. At that time in my life and the affairs of men and women, I was dating a beautiful Protestant girl. As such, she was much more sophisticated than myself.

At the Brock Arena (the present site of Food City), guys and gals could attend stag.

Not so at the new nightclub. It was couples only. If you went to The Aragon on a Saturday eve, as almost everyone did, and another couple happened to join you at your table, you exchanged one dance, never more - in case the other chap might think you were trying to move in on his girl and your upper dentures could be in jeopardy. You didn't dance too closely. If, in a fit of passion, your girl-friend embraced you, you would glance over your shoulder to see if you were being observed. It never happened to me. Well, once I got lucky.

The Aragon was more than a night spot; it was the scene of wedding receptions, political rallies, sponsored balls and service club dinners. Sometimes after such an event, a crap game would break out. One night I was up $200. Drunk with power, I intended to elope with Miss Canada or Bette Davis, whoever was available or passing through. Suddenly Neil Harrington, dean of the gambling fraternity in our town and a cousin of mine, tapped me on the shoulder. "Clare, there is a paid up cab at the entrance. Go home. All hell is about to break loose. And give my regards to your mother." I went home.

The happening: Three pagans from Oshawa had infiltrated the ranks of true Christians, bearing exotic dice - and that, too, was contrary to the code. When the sting became apparent, the bandits fled. The outside chase developed into a highway chase. The result? I can't remember. Sometimes loss of memory can be convenient.

One night, legend has it, Jack Wineberg, in a wild game lost the club to a local physician. The time? Midnight. At 2:35 a.m. he won it back. Both sporting gentlemen are now deceased. Remember I said it was only a legend.

The Aragon served food, but after an evening of dancing, your table usually attended the Paris Café (now The Hi Tops) for Chinese food, a gentle sail down the Yangtze River. Do you know, I never got an encouraging fortune cookie. Once it simply read: "Please ignore previous cookie."

Eventually the era of the Club Aragon came to an end, as God in his wisdom dictates. I never drive by the site (presently Trentwinds) that I don't close my eyes and once again I am swinging at the Aragon and listening to the magic of Sugar Blues, and holding the hand of the Protestant girl.

My Guest The Ghost - Second Visitation

I lay claim to a private ghost. His name is Francis Hinks Dobbin, born 1850, once proprietor of the Peterborough Review, once president of the daily section of the Canadian Press Association - and local historian of renown. He never announces his visits. Just a puff and there he is, himself: tall, slim, white-haired, attired in tailored Victorian splendour, artfully barbered and sporting pince-nez glasses on a neck cord.

In the lexicon of the dictionary, a ghost is the soul of a dead person haunting the living. Sound ominous? Not so with Francis. He is a man of gentle sway and formidable common sense. In his last experienced election, he voted the Conservative ticket, itself the measure of a man.

After a wisp of a handshake, then this opener: "Well, Clare Francis, tell me what's coming down locally." (I'm trying to update his vocabulary.) He continues: "How are our Native people doing?"

I scramble for a reply: "It's a struggle. By the way, just last week the Curve Lake band had a wild game dinner, public invited."

He resumes: "I remember my father telling me that the Mississauga tribe ceded two million acres to the Assembly of Upper Canada, in exchange for an annuity of $3000. Such an arrangement would net heads of families, Fifteen Dollars per annum, in perpetuity, or until the race became extinct, which was a possibility." (This was a formidable real estate caper. As a Canadian, proud of my heritage, I blush visibly and reach for a Prozac.) The Hiawatha Reserve was granted 1550 acres, established in 1834. Others followed: Curve Lake, Scugog and north to Rama.

Now about this time an unusual man appeared on the Hiawatha scene: John William Love, and his name bespeaks his purpose. He became a compatriot, a schoolmaster forever instilling habits of industry, thrift, temperance, as well as social mores. In a letter, Mr. Love refers to a great New Year's feast. The year was 1846. The scene, the same village of Hiawatha. The event was long heralded. Natives came from great distances, through snow-covered forests and frozen trails. Selected settlers were invited.

Previous to this, on such important occasions, women were not permitted at the table. Through the good counsel of Mr. Love, women were not only present, but the first to be seated. Joy and happiness were mirrored on every feminine face. A new franchise!

Now, the bill of fare:

Three fine bear, parts roasted, parts boiled. Four prime deer, cooked in like manner, the deer heads adorning the table. A large hog roasted whole. Two beavers (the tails are a delicacy). Six geese, seven turkeys, other fowl. Fresh fish. A large succulent pie of black squirrel. A barrel of fine flour from Peterborough made into bread. Sweet cakes. Preserves of wild raspberry, strawberry, wild grape, and the fruit of the haw tree.

At repast end, old Chief Paudash gave an elegant address in both languages — native and English, in which he commented on their good fortune attributed to the Great Spirit who had sent them the teachings of Jesus Christ. (The leftovers filled many more baskets than the seven of another feast, a long, long time ago.)

Then another puff - and my guest-ghost is gone. He only visits me when I am alone, minus the incessant clamour of the chatelaine and my dog Bonnie Bluebell. But Mr. Dobbin will be back, for we have much in common.

The back door crashes open. Enter the two lovely ladies in my life, excited at their shopping success. When the jubilance settles to a Christian decibel factor, I hear the familiar question: "Anything happen while we were out?"

My response: "Nothing. Nothing at all. Another quiet, uneventful morning."

And the two conspirators, Francis Hinks Dobbin and myself, both smile inwardly. What devious creatures we are!

Christmas In The Thirties

It is Saturday, three days before Christmas - and I am nine years old. What I am about to tell you, the entire collage of events, happens on this singular day.

I arise at 7 a.m., early, to get my turn in the bathroom. My ablutions are Spartan. The teeth, just the front, no one sees the rear. A splash of water on my face and ears. Wet freckled fingers try to subdue wild hair. I invade my brother's drawer and locate the brilliantine. I'm generous with this product, as a result I look like a reject from central casting.

I pull on my clothes: long underwear, breeks, white shirt, a shrunken wine-coloured sweater, knee-high woollen socks. I look grand!

Because of the rush of the season, Mother serves individual breakfasts. For myself, porridge, Quaker Shredded Wheat muffets in hot milk, three slices of toast slathered with butter, topped with Bee Hive Golden Corn Syrup. I am young and I have an appetite! I can eat the shafts off a bread wagon before or after the trip. I eat so fast I get the hiccups. A brother with a voice like a frustrated auctioneer hollers "Boo" in my ear. It cures me of the hiccups, but now I have a hand tremor.

At 10 a.m. my grandmother arrives. She is accompanied by her son, Rev. Fr. Patrick Galvin. The purpose of the visit: the biennial inspection. Mother has anticipated their arrival and the six kids are sparkling bright. Nevertheless we barely pass muster. As usual, Grandmother portrays an unusual interest in myself, always referring to me as "the article". I ponder why she, such a tiny person, commands absolute awe, but her rapier-like tongue places her in the welter weight class, and a contender to boot. She departs after a cup of tea and one piece of raisin bread. The line-up collectively heaves a sigh of relief.

This year our Christmas tree is glorious. It touches the ceiling. I am not entirely satisfied with the arrangement of the ornaments. For the tenth time I make changes. You see, my standards are very high.

I glance at the clock. I must get to the cathedral for confession to prepare myself for communion come midnight Mass. I enter the vestry. People are lined up outside each booth. Two priests are working backup at the sanctuary railing to ease the pressure. I choose the younger one because I know him. His almost-new stole, emblematic of his office, circles his neck. He is in total command, the liaison between heaven and hell and disputed territories in between.

I cross myself and begin: "Bless me Father, for I have sinned." He interrupts: "I'm sure you have, Clare, but make it brief, tighten it up." My reputation for running on at the mouth has preceded me. Absolution is granted. The penance is modest which is only right. At nine years of age, I am hardly a serial killer, and sex to me is a numeral between five and seven.

Before leaving the cathedral, I visit the crib, and there they are: the Baby Jesus, His parents, the animals and the shepherds. The latter really look great. All that fresh air in the hills of Jerusalem can do wonders.

I run and slide my way home. Christmas is near, no time to dawdle. I pass two sleighs powered by teams of Clydesdales and Percherons. The proud Clydes have ribbons of scarlet around their necks and rosettes on their bridles. There will be no living with them. Occasionally an iron-clad hoof hits a patch of bare pavement and sparks fly. And always the tintinnabulation of bells, bells, bells.

In our kitchen Mother is baking bread, pies and tarts and creating divinity fudge. The smells alone are addictive. I help her knead the dough. Then, like two conspirators, we halt and have a cup of tea. Even at this age I am mad about tea. Plain black Salada is the best.

Now it's hockey time at the Donegal Street free rink. My skates are too small. I borrow my sister's, cunningly inserting a strip of felt between tongue and laces and over the narrow toe cap to conceal their gender. In the shack, the guy next to me says:

"You're wearing your sister's skates." And I say: "You're wearing your big brother's. My god, the size of them! Where do you go to turn around?"

I'm just on time to catch Vespers. With this charge of devotion to Holy Mother the Church, the Pope will probably beatify me when I reach senior fourth - the first in the diocese!

We have a light supper; we are all conserving ourselves for the big feast-day ahead. Everyone disappears. I know my brothers are sparking girls, my sisters are in their room reading Lucy Maud Montgomery and weeping. I help Mom to wash, dry and put away the dishes. She says: "You are a good boy, Clare." Now remembering all this I think of a poem:

"Sometimes I sit alone and think,

How nice 'twould be by far,

If we only were the fellows

Our mothers think we are."

I join my father in the living room. He turns on the Deforest Crosley (even then it was Hockey Night in Canada). Just last summer we installed a new aerial in the garden, a wooden pole higher than the main mast of Sir Walter Raleigh's "Golden Hynde". It works. We crowd closer to the set awaiting the less than dulcet tones of Foster Hewitt. The Maple Leafs ice such players as Hap Day, Charlie Connacher, Busher Jackson, King Clancy, giants in a pygmy world. Despite my excitement, I fall asleep. Dad wakens me: "Go to bed, Lad. You need your rest."

I pull on my nightshirt, then kneel down on the cold floor to say my prayers to the little Baby in the crib. I look out the window. It is snowing. The flakes are big as quarters. I can't see the Christmas star. I remember when I believed in Santa Claus.

The years have passed and the time is now. The chatelaine has trimmed our tree and it is all wrong. Fastidious as she is, she is totally lacking in creativity. Not to worry: "Clare is here!"

But I won't hurt her feelings; I'll wait until the next time she goes shopping and I'll change the entire scene.

And to my readers:

MERRY
CHRISTMAS

from

a kid from the '30s

courtesy of John Lyon

George Street looking north from Charlotte Street. Roy Studio Collection.

Romance In The Fast Lane

The other day while lunching with a friend, for some inexplicable reason I put out the question: "Tell me about your first date?"

He hesitated, then replied: "She was an Italian Catholic girl from Parnell Street. No, it was a girl who lived on Maria Street - a Protestant of Lithuanian heritage. To be honest, I'm not sure." In those days, racial origin and religious persuasion were significant.

To avoid any discomfort, I then said: "Tell me about your first car." A dramatic pause, the eyes misted, he appeared to be gazing into a distant sunrise. This time he spoke with conviction. "It was a 1937 black Plymouth business coupe, grey interior with a white-walled spare tire, heater suspended under the dash, licence number F62 914.

"I spotted this beauty on a used car lot and approached the proprietor, William Hickey, our town's most successful salesman. He could persuade a trout to walk out of the river. Bill took me for a demo ride and never opened his mouth. Some salesman! On our return, he placed the palm of his hand dramatically on the hood of the car like a benediction and said: 'Isn't she a doll?'

"Shouldering him aside, I scurried to the office with $200 cash clutched in my damp hand, the balance promised come Easter time on my grandmother's grave! It was a deal! I hardly slept that night."

I asked that same multiple question to other friends and the scenario was astonishingly similar: the first date, a little vague - the first car, clear as the Liberty Bell.

His Worship Jack (Lefty) Doris: In 1953 Lefty purchased a 1935 black Dodge four-door, the price $150. Knowing how parsimonious his worship can be on occasion, he is probably still driving the same vehicle. In fact, I am certain he is.

Stanley McBride, former mayor, former sheriff: In 1938 Stan purchased a 1925 Star, the sleeve ticket price $35. He did not possess the chariot outright, rather it was owned by a syndicate: the two other executive officers being Will Wildman and Jim Hardy.

Bernard O'Toole, retired from Her Majesty's mail service: In 1939 Bernie bought a green 1929 Chevrolet four-door, price $125. Behind the wheel, he was "*King of the Road.*"

Gordon Farquharson, QC: In 1950 Gordon purchased a spanking new 1950 maroon

Chevrolet two-door. He must have saved his money while serving with the RCAF.

Dr. John Foote: John's first car (purchased in 1949) was a 1936 black Chevrolet two-door. I could not determine the financial arrangements. A very private person.

John W. Corkery, QC: First car was a 1950 green Pontiac two-door, purchased from James Fallen, who, like Mr. Hickey, was persuasive with river trout.

My God, what a revelation! In that era there must have been prevalent hormone deficiency, some dietary lack, maybe a malfunctioning pituitary gland.

Personally, I never enjoyed good health all the days of my life, but the old pituitary never gave me a moment's concern. And while on the subject, did you know that Canada Packers (present site of the Holiday Inn), in the days when they were slaughtering hogs, would remove the pituitary gland from behind the animal's ear with a pea shooter-like device for medical research purposes?

Not remembering your first date is barbaric, unfeeling. It is at the very least less than Christian. Now I remember my first love: gorgeous dimensions, truly an exotic. She was designed by R. Buckminster Fuller who created the American geodesic dome at the 1967 Montreal Expo; she was assembled by Chrysler Dodge Corporation in the nativity year 1935, and deservedly called the Airflow. Due to my youth, only ping-pong table high and naturally in modest financial circumstances, I did not possess her until 12 years down the road, but possess her I did.

This fetching coquette and himself honey-mooned in Algonquin Park. Every morning I scrubbed and polished her. It was an exciting summer. Just now, something prompted me to look out the window at my present auto. How droll!

Have I forgotten my first date? Not at all. Not at all. Tall, ivory complexion, raven hair - or was she blond? *"Ah yes, I remember her well!"*

courtesy of Marlow Banks

1917 Ford owned by C.R. Banks, 314 Maitland Avenue, Peterborough.

New Year's Ramblings

Take a walk backward in time, half a century ago; the year is 1946. The war is over and our boys are home from overseas. Industry has geared up for the consumer market, new automobiles are available in modest numbers, rationing is a thing of the past. Young men are still sporting zoot suits while the ladies gravitate to the "new look" with hemlines just above the ankles (I personally take exception). There is a feeling of national optimism.

New Year's Eve approaches and I am in a quandary. There's a skating party at Artificial Lake below the Pagoda Bridge, with hot chocolate served around a roaring fire. Could do that. Or maybe a movie: The Regent Theatre is showing *The Mysterious Mr. Valentine, at the Centre, Zane Grey's Wanderer of the Wasteland, and at the Capital, Dragonwyck* starring Gene Tierney, Walter Huston and Vincent Price. I am mad about Gene Tierney, in fact I have written to her to see if she would be interested in a meaningful relationship. She hasn't answered my letter.

This evening is very important to me. I have a date with a wildly attractive girl, everything must be right. Perhaps jitter-bugging at the Summer Gardens to the music of Hal McFarlane would be the answer. There'll be balloons, horns, noisemakers and streamers included for just $3.50 a person. Or we could go to the Club Aragon with Del Crary and his band. You can stash booze under the table, and buy your mix for 20 cents a glass. Then again, Jimmy Duffus' orchestra is at The Pines.

It is the morning of December 31. The telephone rings. The mother of "the wildly" calls to tell me that her daughter has a bad chest cold. The date is cancelled.

I decide to honor my great aunt Sarah with my company. She is delighted and says: "I'll tune in the Marconi (radio) and we'll listen to that nice Lombardo boy from London. We do - and we also have butter tarts, Christmas cake and green tea.

I awaken New Year's morning on a chesterfield. Great Aunt Sarah has removed my shoes and covered me with a couple of pink and white afghans. I have a crick in my neck. Portrait of a playboy!

And the time is now:

The Gregorian calendar designates January 1 as New Year's Day. As 1997 makes its stealthy entrance, the second millennium lurks in the corridor. Insurance stats indicate that

I might miss this latter occasion, so for the time available I will take full advantage, grab the ring on the carousel, look for a place in the sun and generally milk the cow with three hands.

It is the season of the year for resolutions, the time to examine one's personal state of the nation. The chatelaine and I share a modest bungalow that we built 39 years ago beside the road beside the lake, where we watch the race of men go by on land and sea. With the years, the dwelling has mellowed, as has our marital relationship.

The third member of the household is Bonnie Bluebell, the clever little creature. We play chess together. She is not *that* clever, however, I can take her two out of three games. I am attempting to raise the Bluebell in the traditions of the Roman Church. The stopper is that the chatelaine kicks with the opposite foot. Some ecumenical arrangement must be made!

My spouse and I share a common pursuit; we like to write. We also act as critics. I criticize her work, she criticizes mine - sometimes a volatile situation. Yesterday she threw her writing pad at me. I nimbly sidestepped to save the sight of both eyes. Now, with the situation reversed, I merely put my notebook aside and retreat into a totally silent snit, a pose that would make Mohandas K. Gandhi seem like a talk show host. We must have a referee, or one of us will end up in the infirmary with a "no visitors" sign on the door. Neither one of us will earn the Governor General's Award. But it is the search for the chalice - therein lies the true adventure.

I try to keep abreast of the times. I'm dancing as fast as I can. You must understand that I was born before TV, computers, disposable diapers, frozen dinners, the pill, group therapy, general absolution, penicillin and mini skirts. Incredible advances have been made in medical science which might account for that persistent feeling that I am dying cured.

I am continually reminded of my mortality. Friends keep dropping off, and sometimes I act as pallbearer, a Christian task. Last week, mounting the church steps with my burden, minus steroids, obviously under physical stress, the chap behind me whispered encouragingly: "Bear up, Clare. Remember, it is better to be on the handles than in the box."

Lately it seems to me that I am forever doing things I don't want to do. In the New Year that must stop. I'm staging a revolt. In the last two days I have reread a history of the American Revolution and perhaps that has served as my inspiration. And in addition, I have no intention of paying the increased tax on tea.

In the future I intend to practise my faith with more fervour to circumvent my parish priest denouncing me from the altar as a "slider".

This year I will resume my fishing career, become predator of the waves again, demon of the deep and regain my reputation as a top angler. God does not deduct from man's life-span the time he spends fishing.

I really should give "Wildly" a call one of these days and check on her chest.

Surely a man of my vintage must have a legacy to leave the younger set, a code. Of course I have: When you brush your teeth, massage your gums. Occasionally glance over your shoulder to see if the others are gaining. Never take yourself too seriously. Never volunteer. Never say YES when you mean NO. And you will be a survivor, as I am. Me, I know! I have survived Mackenzie King, Pierre Trudeau and Brian Mulroney.

New Year's Day is a festival day, the eve celebrated in merriment. It is a time to be with old friends, sing Auld Lang Syne and if you like a 'rub of the brush', nominate a designated driver.

In closing, My New Year's wish to you: "May God keep you in the palm of His hand and never close His fist too tight."

courtesy of Caroline Withers

Celebrating out of town, Brant Inn, Burlington, 1954: from left - Caroline Withers, John Adriaans, Chris Adriaans, Ana Rousell, Spencer Rousell, Bette Galvin, Clare Galvin, Jim Withers.

"How about THAT?"

Good times aboard Compos Mentis 111.

A Day In The Life And Times Of "Himself"

I waken at 6 a.m. I do not require an alarm. I am totally programmed. The girls are still asleep so I put on heavy woollen socks to diminish the decibel factor. Then I don my old terry robe, faded, shredding it's true - but comforting and warm. My day has begun.

I make for the kitchen and plug in the kettle. Then tea in the living room while I watch the dawn pale the blackened skies. Upstage to the east, the day is making its usual apprehensive entrance to reality. I suppose I am the only person in the parish to witness this phenomenon.

I enjoy this early morning interlude. It is a time to plan my day, to think, to reflect. At my age, "the days dwindle down to a precious few", so like a connoisseur, I savour each one. Soon I must prepare breakfast for the two women in my life: the chatelaine and Bonnie Bluebell.

I gaze with chagrin out the window at my lawn and flower beds. We are into the third week of spring and still see the occasional snow flurry. I turn on the news very low so it won't disturb the gals. The soothsayers are vocal but seldom correct, for they inhabit a spot in the Land of Nod, east of the moon. Did you know that our prime minister speaks perfect Anglo? The accent is an affectation. Could Mr. Mulroney be guilty of chicanery, a nice Irish lad like that? I will defend him to the death - his or mine.

I replace the jackets on last night's movies and put them on the shelf where they belong. I am building up a library of classic oldies. I watch these gems over and over, sometimes turning off the sound and supplying the dialogue from memory.

Bonnie Bluebell is up and about. She wants to go out. I snap the lead on her collar and promise the creature that if she plays fast and does not dawdle, a cup of milk will be her reward. She complies.

I finish doing the dishes. I am lusting for an automatic dishwasher, but the chatelaine says they use too much water. With the moneys saved, she has purchased several outfits for herself.

Nowadays, the media are filled with hockey and baseball, the millionaires racing about in their short pants, keeping a sharp eye on the management in the event of a possible injustice. In a past era, they would be playing in an industrial league, their reward at season's end, a nylon club windbreaker and a dinner put on by the Catholic Women's League. I don't wish to sound critical. I never participated in a bodily contact sport. I lie! In years gone by I dated a lot.

Today I will lunch with the guys. I am the singular one who smokes and has a beer, but the paragons are tolerant. This same day, I will drive the perimeters of Ennismore, the township that I live in and love. Since I was a youth, the landscape has altered; shops, subdivisions, restaurants and bars have appeared. When I pass the latter, my car automatically goes into second gear - a custom-built machine equipped with radar. Very expensive, but I never miss a watering hole, thank gawd!

I drive by our new municipal building, the seat of power. The architecture is Greco Roman Colonial. I drop by our federal building (privately owned) and chat with our comely postmistress.

I pick up a few groceries at the general store, then head home to tidy up some more and prepare dinner. This evening, there will be a video and a book. Harrison Ford would not find my day fulfilling. There is a Chinese saying, "May you live in interesting times." It is not a well wish. Rather it is a curse.

At this point you might ask: "But what does the chatelaine contribute?" Well, she does the household accounting and the laundry because she does not trust me in these areas. She is also the resident plumber, great with a can of Draino or the toilet plunger. Before I leave the house, she checks me over to make certain I am suitably attired and unlikely to be apprehended as a vagrant. But mostly she is plugged into her computer, writing the great Canadian novel. Margaret Atwood, hold onto your hat. In addition, she understands me better than I do myself.

Municipal Building, Ennismore Township.

My days are not all identical. Heaven forbid! Rather, they are a moveable feast, a wonderful chest of unexplored drawers to which only I have the key.

PART FOUR

Reflections Of Ireland

During the past quarter of a century, every year I have visited Ireland, the land of my forebears. Although the scenery is beautiful, it is not the sole purpose of my pilgrimages. Rather it is the lure of distant relatives, friends I have made and the charm of the Irish themselves. The Celts are enthralled with eloquence, oral as well as the written word. Their heroes are the poets, the writers. Soccer players are runners-up.

T.E. Kalem, a senior writer for Time Magazine, in his review of *The Borstal Boy* comments:

"The English language brings out the best in the Irish. They court it like a beautiful woman. They make it bray with donkey laughter. They hurl it at the sky like a paintpot full of rainbows, and then make it chant a dirge for man's fate and man's follies that is as mournful as misty spring rain crying over the fallow earth.

"Rarely has a people paid the lavish compliment and taken the subtle revenge of turning its oppressor's speech into sorcery."

As poet laureate, John Masefield stated re England: *"This is the land that free men till, that sober-suited freedom chose... . A man may speak the thing he will. It is unbelievable and inhumane, that England would not extend the same privilege to Ireland. With the Penal Laws and the continued suppression, Naziism is born... ."*

My people emigrated from Listowel, County Kerry, in 1825. Dr. Bryan MacMahon, famed Irish writer and a friend, writes: *"Remember your heritage, we come from County Kerry, the last Kingdom of Ireland, we are not sons and daughters of the flesh, but Children of the Rainbow, dwelling always in the mornings of the world."*

Perhaps this is wishful thinking, but after centuries of oppression, surely it is Ireland's turn for a place in the sun, Ireland's time for a rainbow experience.

Come walk with me, visit places, and listen to the green grass growing and the voices of Ireland.

Eliz Galvin

Old Bridge, County Kerry.

Eliz Galvin

Thatched-roof cottage, Galway Bay.

Flight No. 750 - Destination Ireland

Now I will begin at the beginning. It is mid-evening, Pearson International Airport, Toronto, Canada, with passengers embarking on Flight No. 750, destination Dublin.

Few people are sufficiently observant or gifted to appreciate the mystery and the intrigue such a trans-oceanic passage presents. Our captain comes on the intercom to brief us in both official languages. He speaks neither with evident skill; I wonder what his background is.

The lady honcho announces that this is a "clean air" flight; even the washrooms are monitored to guard against a smoking infraction. To my further dismay she announces there is no bar service, only a light wine is to be served with dinner. Now this scribe is a dedicated smoker and a notorious social drinker. Noting a slight tremor in my right hand and a blurring of vision, I immediately dedicate a prayer to St. Thomas of Aquinas who, in his younger days, was known as a bit of a rounder.

The hand steadies, the eyes clear: "More things are wrought by prayer than this world dreams of." The chatelaine, her head resting on my shoulder, is fast asleep. I have always had this strange narcotic effect upon herself. I remember during our wedding ceremony it took the concentrated efforts of the officiating cleric, the attendants, and myself included to keep her interested in what was transpiring.

The aircraft boasts 12 seats across, with two aisles. When the flight attendants are in motion, pushing their little non-alcoholic carts to and fro, the prospect of visiting a comfort station becomes a fond wish. I bite my lower lip and repeat my mantra. With the help of transcendental meditation and Thomas Aquinas, I just might make it.

Dinner is finally served, chicken cordon bleu flanked with vegetables, but with the lateness of the hour I would willingly settle for a hot dog. The seat is narrow, however, I have a distinct advantage in such close quarters. You see I have the hands and elbows of a gem cutter and I only butter my entire left hand and the crystal of my watch twice. I audibly disdain the wine, explaining to the young women serving the bubbly that I am a recovering alcoholic, at least until I reach Dublin.

The time is 2100 hours, we are 500 miles off the coast of Newfoundland, altitude 30,000 feet, air speed 550 mph, ceiling zero. The latter really doesn't apply, I just thought I would hurl it in for sheer drama!

There is a chap in front of me, late 40s, thinning grey-blond hair, a mite fleshy. He speaks incessantly in an irritating voice to anyone who will lend an ear and even those who don't. His subject: the wife, her virtues, her charms, her beauty, ad infinitum. I decide it must be difficult living with such a paragon. Why didn't he bring her along? The solution comes like a bolt! He has done her in, buried her body in the garden under the chrysanths - and caught the first flight out of town.

I accidentally drop my pen. In retrieving it I notice that each of the flight attendants could qualify for a Hanes lady-of-the-month award. I repeat the drop several times to confirm my first impression. (I never did trust first impressions.)

I observe a mature blond woman, full-figured, dressed in black leather with a fluorescent pink blouse, and wearing enough jewelry to challenge a display window of Tiffany's. As she saunters to the water dispenser she displays a distinct pelvic thrust, undoubtedly a hip problem. Some of the men salute her with a discreet nod. She is either a successful courtesan or involved in politics.

Across from me in an aisle seat is a well-dressed young lad of some ten summers. He buries his head in a book, ignoring everyone around him. Obviously he has been told not to speak to anyone other than staff. He is probably returning home after a term in some private school in Canada, his father an earl of the realm, or at least a belted knight. During the showing of a movie about a team of St. Bernard dogs experiencing the down side of life, I notice tears trickling down his cheeks. These dogs are not carrying the usual flasks under their chins or I would charge the screen. Later the young Fauntleroy falls asleep. An attendant tucks a blanket around him.

In aisle seat G3 is a most attractive lady, fiftyish, shoulder-length raven hair, alabaster complexion, her make-up cunningly applied, her travel suit definitely haute couture. On her left hand she sports a solitaire that challenges the Star of India.

Every time I glance in her direction she rewards me with an encouraging smile. I never kid myself; I am no longer young; many of my manly attributes have disappeared but, I assure myself, those that remain are intensified. I return the smile in kind. When I have an opportunity, I comment to an attendant: "That lady, the one with the raven hair, isn't she most attractive?" And I get this response: "Yes, poor thing, she suffers from a severe form of myopia, can't see a foot in front of her, had to be assisted in boarding." Well, so much for the come-hither smile.

In aisle seat F3 is a slim man, dark, mid forties, black hair slicked back, a slight tic at the corner of his mouth, grey flannel suit, button-down Oxford shirt, mauve tie. Why does he look so familiar? My god, it's Leonard Decatur Keck, the Chatenooga, Tenn., rapist and serial killer. I caught his profile just last week on "America's Most Wanted". Imagine the nerve of the bugger. Of course he hardly expected to encounter myself with the Kodak memory. I could, right now, make a civil arrest. But no! He's a very flaky guy; passengers might be injured, specifically the writer. On landing I'll contact Interpol, and I will get full credit for the collar. Robert Stack will have me on his show as a guest celebrity. Back home they'll have a civic dinner, the family will be invited.

The aircraft touches down on the Dublin tarmac. The young lad, still mute, gathers up his hand luggage across from me and prepares to disembark. The fleshy chap, still talking a blue streak about "the wife" shoulders his way through, unaware that I have it all figured out. I know what's under the chrysanths. The leather-clad blond is not in evidence, no doubt she finally gained access to a washroom. Smiling broadly, the raven-haired beauty passes me by. At my side the chatelaine stirs, yawns and stretches; she can't believe we have arrived.

We de-plane and I am almost on the heels of Leonard Decatur Keck who, surprisingly, is whisked through customs, then met by a liveried chauffeur who relieves him of his attaché case and spirits him away. Hot damn! How could I be so wrong about the guy? So much for my guest appearance on TV, the civic dinner.

The chatelaine, trudging along at my side, comments: "That was a pleasant uneventful trip." You see, only a few rare people share the gift of total perception. I give her a tight smile, the kind that Clint Eastwood tries to emulate, but fails.

I don't tell the chatelaine everything about Flight No. 750. She would only worry.

The O'Sullivan home on Christmas Eve, with a lighted candle in every window.

Irish lad 'On The Wren' plays the spoons.

Christmas In Ireland

It was 7 p.m. on Tuesday, Dec. 19, 1989, when we boarded Wardair Flight No. 101 bound for London, England. Because of a one-hour delay in Toronto, we missed at Gatwick our connecting Dan Air carrier to Dublin. The solicitous Wardair staff looked after our luggage, provided us with a complimentary lunch and secured executive-class accommodation on Aer Lingus.

On our arrival in Dublin's fair city we were the last to disembark because my garment bag had been hung at the rear of the plane. Customs and Immigration, thinking all passengers had been processed, had closed up shop and locked the door. A creative porter loaded our bags on a trolley and led us through two or three store rooms to a taxi stand. Consequently our passports were not stamped and, I suppose, we were in Ireland illegally. However, since it is my wont to mutter, dodder and lurch a bit, no doubt the porter felt confident that I was not a walking delegate to a terrorist convention.

We stayed in a guest house in the residential Iona Park district. It reminded us of a small continental hotel — 20 rooms with all the amenities, a tastefully appointed bar and a gracious dining room at a cost of $92 for two with full Irish breakfast.

While in Dublin we visited "Thornberry" - the 19th century country home of the Crawford family on Marlborough Road. (Isabella Valancy Crawford 1850-1887, one of Canada's great poets, lived in Peterborough for a number of years. She is buried in Little Lake Cemetery and a plaque in her memory stands in Scotts Plains Park across the road from the Peterborough Inn.)

"Thornberry" is now occupied by the Carmelite Order and Rev. Fr. McGoldrick, who met us at the front door, took us through the 14-room house and into a walled garden. It was an unexpected and pleasant tour.

The broad thoroughfare of O'Connel Street in Dublin was a sight to behold. Because of the Christmas season, hundreds of trees on the central boulevard were lighted in white and the whole scene resembled a fairy fantasy.

We boarded the train at Heuston Station for a four-hour journey westward across the country to County Kerry and Tralee. The cost of a single return fare - $46 Canadian. A hamburger in the dining car sold for $8 as opposed to $4 at the airport.

The train was modern and fast. From our window we could see green fields and little cottages and, in the small towns, the railway stations all painted with the same bright blue trim.

The coaches were packed, but the conversation seemed unusually subdued. These people were going home to their villages, to their farms, to their families - it was a time for contemplation and quiet anticipation.

We were met at the station in Tralee by Annette, 21, and William, 19, both students and the children of our hosts, Maureen and Toddy O'Sullivan. Then, for 30 minutes, we motored through driving rain to their spacious Georgian-style farm home just outside Listowel, the area from whence my people emigrated in 1825 among the Peter Robinson group who gave our town, Peterborough, the impetus to fulfil her destiny. Annette was at the wheel. I sat beside her in the Citroen, clutching my rosary in my side pocket. Does everyone in Ireland have to drive as though qualifying for the Players 100s at Mosport?

Maureen and Toddy, their three dogs, and Blackie, the house cat, were waiting at the threshold to greet us. Their welcome was as sincere as the Sermon on the Mount. There were two Christmas trees - one in the parlour and one in the sitting room, and a turf fire glowing in the fireplace. One could feel the warmth and it wasn't just the turf.

During the days remaining before Christmas, I went into Listowel alone and walked the streets of my ancestors. I visited the church where I studied the almost life-sized manger scene. Occasionally, I dropped into a pub and tried one, hoping to encounter someone who might talk a little treason. Many of the bars were small, almost tiny. In one such pub, I observed the only other customer, a contemporary in age, ruddy complexion, tweed cap, in a thoughtful mood, labouring away on his pipe and staring at nothing in particular.

I smiled, engagingly I hoped, and commented on the minuteness of the licence. He agreed that it was indeed. Moments passed; then I enquired, "My gawd, where do you go if a fight breaks out?"

He gazed at me with some puzzlement, then replied: "Sure lad, can't you appreciate the sheer wonder of the situation - you wouldn't miss a thing."

One day on my journeys, a young lad of some nine years (a tinker) wearing a sky-blue toque, stepped in front of me with his palm extended and asked if I would be kind enough to contribute 50 pence to further his Christmas. And in the spirit of the season, I did! Two hours later, and four blocks away, he accosted me again. I reminded him that I had already given. He denied this, saying: "Did the fellow have a blue cap like me?" I replied: "He did." He responded: "Well, that would be my brother."

I gave him another 50p.

While in town, I had the pleasure of having tea with Bryan McMahon. Bryan, a retired school master of some 80 years, appears 20 years younger. This gentleman is a renowned Irish writer and much venerated in the whole of Ireland.

John B. Keane, also a resident of Listowel, is a former student of McMahon's. Keane is a novelist and playwright of some fame, and his play, "The Field", was made into a movie starring Richard Harris. These men, McMahon and Keane, are two of the reasons that Writers' Week is held in Listowel - the town abounds in the creative.

Christmas Eve came and lighted candles were placed in every window of the house, where they would remain until Jan. 6, Little Christmas. I informed Toddy that we would like to attend Midnight Mass. Toddy advised me that Midnight Mass was celebrated at 10 p.m. I enquired: "How come?" Toddy hastened to explain that the monseigneur, in his wisdom, deemed it circumspect to begin a little earlier, thus eliminating the possibility of a segment of the congregation becoming too jarred to fully appreciate the significance of the occasion.

Following Mass we returned to "Derry" to feast, to dance and to sing Christmas carols before the turf fire. It was 4 o'clock in the morning when we finally said our good-nights and went to bed.

Then Christmas morning. The big day arrived with presents being distributed and everyone admiring a Waterford crystal bowl given to Maureen by Annette. A turkey, big as an albatross, began to send out a wonderful aroma from the kitchen; the gammon (ham), covered with pineapple slices and maraschino cherries sat on the table. There was stuffing and Brussels sprouts and turnip and peas and mashed potatoes and gravy and wine - and at the end of the meal, a plum pudding with knee-high blue brandy flames. Then cousins came visiting. Then we visited cousins. What hospitality! What friendships!

The following day, St. Stephen's Day, Dec. 26, was "the day of the wren". People with blackened faces, dressed in costume, carolled and entertained their neighbours, seeking money to "bury the wren" (now, money for charity). This custom dates back, perhaps, to the time of the druids.

At ll a.m. two young men arrived. One played the tin whistle like I didn't know it could be played - and his brother played the spoons, up and down his arms, and off his fingertips. They were truly accomplished, and our host joined them on the bodhran (goatskin drum). Others arrived, but they were less talented.

About 10 o'clock that evening we donned our costumes and "went on the wren". We hit all the bars in Listowel. Annette and William both played the accordion, Maureen and Annette clog-danced, and the rest of us sang - not well, but in the bars they were less than critical. We collected 40 Irish punts!

On Dec. 27 we again boarded the train for Dublin. With tears, hugs and a sprinkling of holy water, our friends saw us off at the station in Tralee. The holiday had ended as all holidays must.

Our trip home was wearisome: four hours across Ireland, a flight to Gatwick in England, a three-hour wait, a seven-hour crossing, the hassle of Toronto airport, then a three-hour trip to Ennismore by Century Airline Service in fearsome driving conditions. But we were home.

I shall continue my love affair with Ireland and her people, but it is in Canada where my forebears sought sanctuary where my heart truly belongs. It is my land. My home.

A Town Called Kilkee

When we arrive in Ireland, we usually head for a town called Kilkee, where we spend several days acclimatizing and overcoming jetlag. Then, before our return to Canada, once again we seek this favoured location to recuperate from the rigours of our holiday and to absorb the atmosphere of one of our special Irish haunts.

This townsite is located on the southwest coast in County Clare, freshened by the breezes from the Atlantic in front and warmed by the waters of the River Shannon to the rear. Kilkee is a summer resort, a spa, dating in popularity back to the Victorian era. Our B & B, "Westcliff House", overlooks the promenade, the strand, and faces the bay and the surrounding cliffs, which are pocked with huge caverns known as the Elephant Caves. Dominating the view is the outermost cliff where nature's hand has carved the caricature of a countenance dubbed "George's Head", in tribute to the monarch so named. George III (1738-1820) experienced some physical and emotional problems and unfortunately sulpha drugs and Prozac were not readily at hand, so for 30 years this king enjoyed periods of insanity before he was eventually declared "out to lunch" and replaced by a regent. The face of the cliff captures his image and tells his story.

This holiday town has been the scene of numerous shipwrecks. To my right is Edmond's Point, clearly visible. In the year 1847, a sailing vessel *"The Edmond"* putting out from Limerick, destination America, emerged from the Shannon River to confront an Atlantic gale so severe the ship sought the refuge of Kilkee harbour, only to founder on the reefs. The townspeople, with their tiny curraghs, attempted to rescue the 200 souls on board, and 100 lives were saved. The following day 100 dead bodies washed ashore and lined the strand of this town.

Another sailing vessel, *"The Intrinsic"*, carrying pig iron to the new world, also foundered on the shoals. An Anglo-Irish gentleman by the name of Sykes, witnessed the happening from an upper-floor window of his mansion. He directed his manservant to alert the villagers. Nothing could be done. The sea was wild. A Catholic priest improvised an altar among the rocks on shore and celebrated Mass within view of *"The Intrinsic"* and her crew huddled on the tilting dock. There were no survivors.

Subsequently, in the next decade, two sailing frigates of the Royal Navy sank off the same coastline. In contrast to the gentle people of the community, there were always the "wreckers", the scavengers who attended the scene of such disasters to glean what they could.

But back to the present. This trip has not been without problems. The chatelaine has developed a dreadful cold and an accompanying cough that sounds like "Sharky" the seal of Marineland fame. I pause in my script to throw another blanket over her, not for comfort, but to muffle the bark. I, myself, have been plagued with a sore and swollen foot. Three nights ago, at a B & B in Kenmare, two English female doctors, noticing my pronounced limp, volunteered to examine the extremity. Their conclusion - gout! I had a gut feeling that they were both gynaecologists, and what would the likes of them know about manly afflictions. On our arrival at Kilkee, I sought the attention of Dr. Nolan, a proper male practitioner. His diagnosis - gout! Before he could embark on the attractions of leading a monastic life, I enquired if visiting historical ruins and damp churches could have instigated this malady. His response: "Everything is possible in the creative mind of man. In this instance, however, I would attribute the condition to an excessive life style." Hot damn! I travel 3,000 miles to discover the word is out on me!

Diana Martin, Westcliff's gracious proprietor, taps gently on our door. She has brought a tea tray. She is concerned about the chatelaine. Am I looking after her? What would we like for dinner? She is going shopping. Can she pick up anything for us? Some cough medicine? Buckley's?

I gaze out the window, the afternoon tide is coming in, a small green and white trawler with a crew of three chugs down the bay. It is mackerel time. I get the field glasses for a better look.

A mother pushes a pram along the promenade - the cargo, a team of redheads. I knock on the window; she looks up. I give the universal sign of approval - a circled thumb and finger. She smiles, waves. I'm glad I knocked.

Schoolboys go by, their bags slung over their shoulders. Through the partially raised window, I catch their dialogue - not the pursuit of the day, but how Ireland will fare in the World Soccer Cup.

An older couple stroll by, their conversation spirited. He puts his arm over her shoulder, she smiles upward. You see: It IS a many-splendored thing!

Two Jack Russell dogs - buddies - perambulate by, glancing about with an air of proprietorship, as if they had a handle on the affairs of the parish.

Soon the lights will appear in those Victorian houses, and the shops and the pubs along the strand - like a string of Christmas tree lights. The chatelaine is breathing a little easier, the anger in my foot has subsided. Mine hostess has lent me a copy of Pride and Prejudice. I will have a nightcap now, and go to bed with Jane Austen, and I will remember a place called Kilkee all the days of my life and perhaps afterwards - and it's kinda nice getting to know Jane intimately once again.

"Schoolboys go by, their bags slung over their shoulders."

Kenmare Bay

"Down the road, keep to the right, through the gate, be sure to relatch it, and you can't miss it - the stone cottage."

A Town Called Kenmare

We arrived in early summer at our arranged B & B, Dunkerron Lodge, Sneem Road, Kenmare, County Kerry. The ivy-covered stone walls, the white wrought-iron entrance gateway, the wooded walks, the wealth of flowers everywhere added charm and a subdued voice of welcome. The six-bay shining windows of this Victorian mansion standing proud on the Ring of Kerry, adjoining the Beara peninsula, echoed that same welcome.

A few hundred feet from the front entrance we could see the ruins of a 15th century castle, once the stronghold of the O'Sullivan-Mor clan (we were told), masters of the area - but no more.

We were greeted by the proprietor, Moya Gubbins, a mature charming self-confident woman. One glance and you knew she had a handle on the situation. Her salutation was: "How are things in Brussels?"

I assumed this was some kind of password. You see, if you grew up in the west end of our town and attended a separate school, you were naturally exposed to a myriad of secret societies and enclaves. I did not attempt a response!

Surprisingly, Moya directed us: "Down the road, keep to the right, through the gate, be sure to relatch it, and you can't miss it - the stone cottage."

Now this dwelling was about 200 years old, but the interior had been modernized to resemble something from *Country Homes & Gardens*. There were two bedrooms and a bath on the upper level, and on the ground level a kitchen and living room boasting a walk-in fireplace. As well there were fireplaces in every bedroom, although electrical radiators were also in evidence.

We were astonished. Did we share the cottage with someone else? Surely not!

From the threshold we could see across Kenmare Bay to the Caha Hills and the Muxnaw ford where the pigs swim. (We had been told that pigs being taken to market, shortened their journey by swimming across the bay).

I mixed a highball to steady the hand and lend a little logic to the situation. Suddenly the chatelaine exclaimed: "I love it. We can have breakfast at the lodge; it's included in the price, and we can have a gorgeous turf fire - the wood box is full - and we can shop in the village and have dinner here! It's great. I can't believe it. Do you suppose the main lodge is completely booked?"

When we returned to the manor house, Moya was profuse in her apologies. We were not the guests from Belgium destined to occupy the quaint cottage. We were, instead, moved upstairs to a large room overlooking the golf course and the bay.

It was in this room that I had my first experience with a down duvet. Covered in blue flowered cotton, it was charming to look at and initially, warm and comfy. But it was an elusive bugger, prone to creep and slide. I was either roasting or freezing to death. When I awakened shivering in the morning, the duvet was six feet from the bed. The following night I double-bolted the bedroom door to make sure the creature didn't escape entirely.

Perhaps in contrition, Moya arranged with her chef to have a special dinner for us that first evening. The curtain raiser was hot grapefruit splashed with sherry, followed by cream of leek soup, fresh salmon steak, creamed potatoes, boiled onions, broccoli and a salad. The dessert, I never did identify; it still remains a mystery - but delicious. Despite the wonder of the repast, the chatelaine was inordinately subdued, she missed the prospect of a week in the enchanted cottage. My natural wit and charm, which usually could cause a pit-bull to lie down and roll over in sheer ecstasy, had lost its magic.

After dinner in the drawing room before a blazing fire (no turf fire here) in the company of two couples representing the Netherlands and South Africa, our hostess recited poetry from the works of W.B. Yeats. During a break, inspired by patriotism and fortified with Irish coffee, the tipsy grapefruit and several cocktails, this writer felt it necessary to embark upon a dozen readings from the Canadian Robert Service. The chatelaine was not amused. The adult beverages were beginning to affect my normally sound judgement. Thank God for the chatelaine. Without her, I would never be accepted in civilized society. We retired.

From our bedroom windows we could see the hills above the blue water of Kenmare Bay. It was easy to understand why this area is said to be one of the most idyllic in Ireland.

The castle ruins intrigued us and we investigated. This Tudor structure was reconstructed in 1450 from an Anglo-Norman fortress by the grandson of Rodericus of the Fair Mair O'Sullivan Mor. It was burned during the Cromwellian wars to prevent it from falling into the hands of the invaders.

The estate eventually became the property of the Taylor family. Joseph Taylor was land agent for Lord Lansdowne who had extensive holdings in Counties Kerry and Cork. This gentleman sponsored a small Irish emigration in 1841 to what is now Peterborough

County. A later Lord Lansdowne served as governor general 1885-1888. Lansdowne Street, that busy thoroughfare in our town, is named in commemoration of this family.

The next day we walked the two sloping downtown streets (which vie for the title of "main"), past the numerous pubs and shops, delighted to find and buy some locally-crafted pottery, and ending up at Quill's Woollen Market where you can purchase just about anything Irish.

At the top of the street is the impressive grey stone Park Hotel where the tariff per night, double, is $450(Canadian). Quite beyond the means of a township lad. "Couldn't we just have tea?" the chatelaine pleaded. Who could refuse such a simple request? And so we enjoyed open-face, smoked salmon sandwiches, the tea, of course, for 22 Irish punts; that's $44 Canadian, or just about. It was grand.

Strolling back to the town square we noted a young chap standing on a corner with a brown and white pony tethered beside him on the road, a "for sale" sign around the neck of the pony. Neither boy nor pony looked too happy at the prospect of a sale.

Sitting on the stone fence of the village park we watched the bustle of the farmers' market. Around us were rose trees taller than Magic Johnston. On the pretence of finding a washroom, I slipped into Quinn's Bar to quaff a cold ale. I'm a devil.

I visit the Convent of the Poor Clares, just off the square behind the cathedral. I press the bell. There is no response. Probably the girls are at prayer. I leave negotiable alms in the box. With my name, Clare, and the severe tribulations of my lifetime, surely on request I would qualify as an affiliate member of the order. I try the buzzer once more. Nothing. Perhaps they saw me coming.

We trudge up an incline of one of the streets back to our auto. On the slope I make a pledge. Some day, God willing, we will return. I will arrange with Moya Gibbins to rent the enchanted cottage for a week. We will breakfast at the lodge, shop for provisions in the village, and have dinner before a turf fire in the walk-in fireplace. That will make the chatelaine happy, and once again she'll be entranced with my wit and charm.

If this can be arranged, and if you should have reason to contact me during this time, you might try Dunkerron Lodge, the stone cottage, or call the Convent of the Poor Clares and ask for the affiliate. I'll be out in the garden with the rhododendrons.

I must go now. I hear the bell for vespers.

Clare meets Irish President Mary Robinson.

Clare with author Bryan MacMahon.

Writers' Week In Ireland

This year, the chatelaine and "himself" had the pleasure of attending the 21st celebration of Writers' Week in Ireland (May 24 - June 2, 1991).

In January, I received a letter from Dr. Bryan MacMahon, renowned Irish writer, encouraging me to actively participate in the affair, and to give a lecture on *The Holy Land (Ennismore)*, and the story of the Peter Robinson emigration in 1825 to the Peterborough area of Upper Canada. My disdain for the limelight and my natural shyness compelled me to decline.

The week was designed to create a climate of awareness in which writing, both in Irish and English, could flourish and be exhibited. This moveable feast now manages to touch most bases: music, drama, poetry readings, art exhibitions, book fair, book launchings and workshops. As well, there are literary tours and historical tours. The event is of national importance, shouldering on the international, and it is located in the market town of Listowel, on the banks of the River Feale, once in the kingdom and now in the county of Kerry.

The setting is fittingly chosen as it is the home of Ireland's two most famous living writers: Bryan MacMahon, author of numerous works including *Children of the Rainbow*; and the prolific John B. Keane, whose story The Field became a movie, starring Richard Harris who was nominated that year for an academy award.

MacMahon and Keane, each with his own particular style and genius, powers of perception and compassion, have captured the colour, the lore, the very heart and soul of what this fabled land is all about. We had met both John B. Keane and Bryan MacMahon on previous visits, and we were pleased to be warmly greeted. (Visit your favourite bookstore. Pick up a volume written by Keane or MacMahon. I promise you will go back to the well again and still again.)

Other unforgettable Listowel sons are: Sean McCarthy, deceased within the year, famous for his poetry, ballads and stories; and Maurice Walsh, creator of *The Quiet Man*.

At the opening gala dinner, Ireland's President Mary Robinson was the guest of honour. We had the pleasure of being introduced to this gracious woman.

One evening, we saw Nora Relihan as a powerful sole performer of Brian

Merriman's 18th century *The Midnight Court.* This drama, written entirely in verse, deals with the social problems of marriage, divorce, contraception, priestly celibacy, and the role of the church in society - issues that no longer disturb our enlightened and sophisticated thresholds (wouldn't you say?).

At the Sean McCarthy memorial evening we were entertained by Carmel Quinn, who starred years ago on the Arthur Godfrey Show on radio, and appeared for 30 consecutive years at Carnegie Hall, the single performer who can make such a claim. With her thrilling voice and charming manner, she defies the challenge of time. We were fascinated by a dozen mature women in Irish costume who illustrated what clog dancing should sound and look like. There wasn't a steady boot in the house. Then came the Listowel Singers, a 35-member mixed choir who enchanted us with their gifted voices in renditions of melodies, old and new. They had also charmed audiences in the United states and gave a command performance for the Supreme Bishop of Rome. Their final number, *"New York, New York",* jarred the rafters.

On Thursday morning, May 30, we had a visit from the secretary of Writers' Week. She informed us that Dr. MacMahon had specifically requested we attend the 11:00 a.m. lecture being held in St. John's Square. It seemed Eamon Dunphy's lecture "Coming to Journalism Late in Life" had been cancelled, and Dr. MacMahon and Gabriel Fitzmaurice had agreed to fill in. There was a daylight rumour about, endorsed by a sound truck, that in addition there was to be a mystery guest. The mystery guest turned out to be "Himself" from Canada. Sensing the atmosphere, I took a pill, quaffed a rum and mumbled a prayer to St. Jude. Now, whereas I did not have the audience rolling in the aisles, neither did I bring discredit upon my house It was Jude who carried the day, also the rum didn't go amiss.

During the week there was a certain amount of celebrity hunting. One day, while window-shopping, I turned abruptly and crashed into a woman. In the midst of my apology, she asked: "Are you Richard Harris, the famous movie star?" Responding in the negative, I said: "If you examine me once again, you'll find I'm much more handsome." Retreating a pace, she scrutinized me closely and said: "Meaning no offence, sir, but you're not!"

Sometimes, during the week, I would make a visit to St. Mary's Roman Catholic Church modestly tucked to one side of the square. The chatelaine, though of a different persuasion, always accompanied me to keep an eye on my whereabouts. One day, out of the corner of my eye, I noticed her surreptitiously lighting a candle. Members of the protestant faith are forever hedging their bets - may God have mercy on their tiny souls.

It is difficult to recreate the excitement of the week: the hurry, the emotional charge, the desire to participate in everything. Between sessions everyone rushed to a pub for a pint, or a pot of tea and a smoked salmon sandwich. Friends gathered together. New friends were made. Those who were involved in workshops groaned about their assignments.

Typewriters could be heard pounding away in the rooms. Poetry readings were held at midnight, and sing-alongs at the Listowel Arms until God knows what hour. It was impossible to see everything, do everything. Those who tried were easily recognized on the thoroughfares - the descriptive line would read: *"And the dead arose and appeared to many!"*

We came home with memories of sharing an evening with poet Anne Hartigan who had just returned from reading her work in New York City, and with Alice Taylor of *Quench the Lamp* fame. Heady stuff!

My people emigrated from this town, this Listowel, these very banks of the River Feale. Under desperate circumstances they left this land 170 years ago. Now, it is good to go back and visit the old town, to be greeted and entertained by people of the Galvin name, tenuous as the relationship might be.

I love my country, Canada, but I'm proud also that once upon a time my people came from an exalted kingdom, the Kingdom of Kerry and I am one of the children of the rainbow!

Clare with Mary and John B. Keane (author The Field).

photo by Leo Howran

. . March 17th Peterborough Irish Breakfast Club at Tavana's, 394 George Street north - 1984. Front row from left: Ken Dormer, Jack Duggan, Stan McBride, Frank McCarthy. Back row from left: Fred Gariepy, Lorne Collins, Clare Galvin, Terry O'Keefe, John Corkery, Keith Brown.

The banner was designed by Fred Gariepy. It is Kelly green with orange lettering (the colours of Ireland). In the centre, there is a tank, not unlike a storage tank, and to either side of the tank, a leprechaun is deep in thought in the configuration of Rodin's ***The Thinker****. In Fred's words:"The motto is self-explanatory and although the reference is to the Peterborough Canadian Irish Club, the Think Tank, like a rump Parliament, stands or more precisely sits alone, an entity unto itself."*

THE PETERBOROUGH CANADIAN IRISH CLUB
SATURDAY MORNING
THINK TANK
"Canadian First Irish Always"
EST. 1976

Clare hosts March 17th Irish Breakfast at Buddy's Place in Ennismore, 1994. Clare in white sweater. To the right: Fred O'Grady, John Foote, Richard Batten and Ralph Standish.

Saturday morning, Peterborough Irish Breakfast Club. From left: Clare Galvin, Frank McCarthy, Stan McBride, Keith Dinsdale, Barry O'Sullivan, Fred Bartley, Tony Ross, John Corkery and Fred Gariepy.

Of Cabbages, Convicts, Harps And Festivals

I am not aware of any city in this trillium Province of Ontario where the Irish immigrants have made such a profound contribution to growth, culture and economy as in Peterborough itself.

In the year 1825 there was only a handful of settlers in our locale. With the British assisted immigration from Ireland that same year, under the direction of Peter Robinson, the palm of the hand swelled with 2025 souls. Even today, in pockets of our county, 170 years later, the touch of Celtic brogue is still pleasantly evident.

The Irish, generally, made good citizens in their adoptive countries. An account attributed to W. George Hodgson, published in the Congressional Record, Washington (date unavailable), has been brought to the writer's attention. What follows is not verbatim, but rather the 'gist of the thing'.

In the Ireland disorders of 1848, nine young men were arrested, convicted of treason and sentenced to be hanged by an English court. The presiding judge read out their names: Charles Duffy, Morris Lyene, Patrick Donaghue, Thomas D'Arcy McGee, John Mitchell, Thomas Meagher, Richard O'Gorman, Terrance McManus and Michael Ireland.

World-wide protest moved Queen Victoria (not famous for being an easy mark) to commute the sentences to banishment in the penal colony of Australia.

In 1871 a Charles Duffy was elected Prime minister of the Australian state of Victoria. When the astonished monarch was informed that Duffy was one of the 'notorious nine' sentenced to the penal colony, 23 years earlier, she demanded to know what had happened to the remaining eight.

Impressive records emerged: Terrance McManus and Patrick Donaghue were both brigadier generals in the army of the United States; Richard O'Gorman had become Governor of Newfoundland; Morris Lyene, former attorney general of Australia had been succeeded by Michael Ireland; Thomas D'Arcy McGee was president of the Council for the Dominion of Canada; John Mitchell was a prominent New York politician, and Thomas Meagher was Governor of the State of Montana. A laudable record for a bunch of convicts.

Just about now the reader might suspect this scribe of being a tad proud of his own Celtic origin and is blowing his own tin whistle. Well, I ask you - why not? As my sainted grandmother so often said: "It's a dumb priest that can't get his own parish."

On an illustrious monday evening, July 7th, 1975, to be exact, a group with Irish ancestry held a meeting at our county courthouse and gaol. The purpose of this meeting was to select a slate of officers for the newly-formed Peterborough Canadian Irish Club. Perhaps the key members considered for executive positions were experiencing brief periods of incarceration (I do have a tendency to dramatize) - perhaps they were merely there for interrogation. One can only speculate.

President	John Corkery, QC
Vice-president	Stanley Armstrong McBride
Secretary	Terrance O'Keefe
Treasurer	Mary Amyotte

The thrust of the organization was, and is, to keep alive the Irish heritage. Another credo: Members are neither Roman Catholic nor Protestant, neither North nor South - just everyone 'grandly green'.

Now, to matters at hand. The annual Irish Festival will be held at the Douro Community Centre, Highway 134, on Saturday, June 4. Doors will open at 12 noon. There will be Irish imports for sale, genealogy information available, displays, entertainment, food and free parking. At 8 p.m. Ethna Heffernan, renowned Irish harpist and singer, will present her concert which is to be followed by dancing to the music of Tom O'Donaghue and Edna O'Brien and band. The special drawprize is return airfare to Ireland. The admission price is incorrigibly modest. Older residents of our community can become re-acquainted with our Irish roots. Newcomers - well, let me introduce you! I promise you that there will not be a mean face in the crowd nor a steady boot in the house.

Unaccustomed as I am to proffering dispensations. But God willing:

"May the wind be always at your back,

May the sun shine warm on your face.

May you be in heaven, one half hour

Before the devil knows you're dead!"

March 17 - Irish Memories

March 17 is closing in, the time of year when more than usual I choose to think about Ireland, with St. Patrick, of course, foremost in my thoughts.

St. Patrick, the patron saint of Ireland C. 385-461 was born in Britain. As a youth he was kidnapped by Irish marauders and enslaved. For six years he served as a herdsman and eventually escaped to Gaul. Because he had a vision, which called him to return to Ireland to Christianize that country, he became a priest. In 431, after the death of St. Palladius, the first missionary bishop sent to Ireland, Patrick was consecrated by Pope Leo I and sent to that land (432).

In my readings, historians invariably comment on Patrick's winning personality. However, I have my own composite of the man himself. To make Christians out of the pagan Irish would have required the patience of our current pope, John Paul, the humour of Roger Dangerfield and the stamina of a heavyweight champion plus a steady hand on the throttle.

Each spring for the past many years, this writer has visited Ireland, that land of 40 shades of green and a thousand welcomes. I knock on the door of a modest cottage; it opens, I smell the turf fire, and a man I haven't seen in 10 years is there to greet me: "Glory be to God, it's yourself Clare Francis Galvin. I wouldn't have recognized you. You haven't changed a bit!" And the process begins. The scenery in Ireland is breathtaking, but it is the dialogue that I most enjoy. When I return, I walk the streets of this market town and I am often greeted with the salutation: "Top of the day to you, Mr. Gallivan." I find the experience a tad disturbing. One would think that after more than 170 years (when my relatives emigrated from Ireland to Ennismore Township) we would have improved in appearance.

Getting back to the dialogue. The following are some maxims that continue to amuse me:

"Get down on your knees and thank God you are on your feet."

"You can accomplish more with a kind word and a shillelagh, than you can with simply a kind word."

"There comes a time when you must take the bull by the tail and face the situation squarely."

And a favourite of mine, perhaps because I am nearing the finishing line myself: "We drink to your coffin; may it be built from the wood of a 100-year-old oak tree, that I shall plant tomorrow."

This past year, during the bottom of May and the top of June, I continued my romance with Ireland.

Motoring in that land of narrow twisting roads, where one is obliged to steer and drive on the wrong side, is indeed a challenge. With brilliant forethought, I purchased two large "L" decal signs, which I pasted to my front and rear windshields (or windglass, as they call it), thereby alerting all fellow motorists that they were dealing with a learner - or a lunatic. The plot worked! Only once in the three weeks that I (no doubt) caused terror on the byways, did a driver sound his horn in criticism of my navigational skills. This occurred as I attempted to find an exit from Galway City.

A tailing motorist started blasting his horn. Through the open window on my side of the car, I extended 'the finger', a gesture universally recognized since the crusades. What did he do? He overtook us, and had the audacity to crowd us curbside. With my adrenalin flowing and ready for action, I emerged from my vehicle at the same time as he did. My God, he looked like a pale George Foreman; I immediately fell into a crouch with a noticeable bob and weave. At my age, my only chance was to kill him with my footwork. He raised his right hand, palm open, in the American Plains Indian symbol of peace with a desire to parlee. I made two more devastating practice hooks to the west with the wind and listened.

"Sir," he said, "I am sorry to impede your progress, but your boot has become ajar and you are in danger of losing your luggage."

I quietly mumbled my thanks and returned to my car, walking forward on my toes, with my forearms raised, in a manner reminiscent of John Wayne. My wife, having heard nothing of the exchange was tremendously impressed with my manly ways. The fact that I had the hiccups for the next 15 minutes only slightly marred this image.

We stayed for several days in Kilkee, County Clare. Extending west from Kilkee is the Loop Head Peninsula, with the hamlet of Kilbaha and the Church of Moneen. For specific reasons I wanted to visit this area, and I followed the directions of Diana Martin, our hostess at Westcliff House.

It was misty when we embarked along the Cliff Road, the scenic route (God deliver me from scenic routes) - then, suddenly, the mist lifted, and I was confronted with a yellow warning roadsign showing a car going over a cliff, headed for the briny deep.

Now, I experience a mild form of vertigo - nothing crippling. But suddenly there I was, five feet from a precipice, with the wild Atlantic dashing against the cruel black rocks below. Not to panic. I brought the auto to a halt, engaged the emergency brake, lurched out of the vehicle, and fell to my knees. Then, mumbling religious incantations, clutching the turf and digging in my toes, I worked my way around to the far side of the car. The chatelaine was there to greet me, dust me off, and propel me into the rear seat of the Nissan, whereupon she handed me my rosary, threw a topcoat over my head as usual and assumed the wheel. In the welcome darkness, the balance of the trip was uneventful.

Now the reason for this journey: In the year 1852, the English Penal Laws were still casting their dark shadows across certain areas of Ireland. Father Meehan, the parish priest in the Loop Head, did not have a church. Residents of the locality had been warned that if they permitted mass to be celebrated in their homes, the landlords would evict them, and their houses would be destroyed.

Father Meehan had a carpenter construct a two-wheeled mini-caravan, with windows on three sides, an altar at one end and a short step-ladder leading to an open doorway. The Roman Catholic faithful had their church. On Sundays and on holy days of obligation, the vehicle was pulled to the beach and placed on that strip of sand between the high tide mark and the low tide mark - that strip that no man-made law dares govern.

The peninsula now boasts a proper church - the Church of Moneen. On the epistle side, near the sanctuary, the mortal remains of Father Meehan are interred. To the left of the main altar, in a small outer room also used as the church baptistry, the Little Ark was placed. There it remains. Father Meehan and his worm-eaten, weather-beaten caravan to heaven, resting in peace.

I glanced out a window to the sloping meadows with their glorious wild flowers spreading down to the sea. It was peaceful there on the Loop Head - the tyrants, long gone.

There are many reasons I return to Ireland again and still again. It is the people. Simply asking directions can be an experience. "See that road over there? Ignore it completely. It won't do you a bit of good. Turn right before you encounter the pharmacy, and if you miss that, turn right at Cronyn's Bar."

And the bar scene is something I must touch upon. The legend of drinking Irish is over-emphasized. In all my visits, I recall seeing only one drunken individual, and that was a woman. A man sits in a pub with his pint of Guinness at hand and it will last him all evening. He is there for the conviviality, not for the booze.

Some day, you, Madam/Sir, must visit Ireland, the land of one thousands saints and scholars, the turf, the goblins, leprechauns, fairies, the land of St. Patrick, himself.

To quote Yeats:

"I am of Ireland,

And the Holy Land of Ireland,

And time runs on," cried she.

"Come out of charity,

Come dance with me in Ireland."

An Irish pub with Maura Galvin.

PART FIVE

BACK BY POPULAR REQUEST

Verandah Society

Webster's Dictionary defines a verandah as "an open portico or gallery usually roofed and sometimes partly enclosed, attached to the exterior of a house or other building." When I was a kid in the '30s, almost every home boasted such a gallery, and it contributed much to the social scene during the summer months.

I was born in the two-storey frame house at 461 Murray Street, just west of Park. My parents purchased this dwelling in the roaring '20s for the grand sum of $2,200. They had saved money for a substantial down payment and they were further assisted by a local building and loan society.

Our house had one helluva verandah that ran the full width of the house. And with nine in the family, we needed it all. The eastern end was latticed and embraced by a Dutchman's Pipe vine which provided a private bower. The balance was open to the entire world. A half dozen chairs were properly spaced across the porch, and more could be brought from the kitchen if the occasion demanded. It often did.

In the evenings after supper, my father would take his pipe to the verandah. When the dishes were done, Mother would hang up her apron and join him. One by one the young fry would filter out to occupy the remaining chairs which were allotted by seniority. The last-born sat on the steps.

Across the road in the Albion field, a perpetual scrub-softball game would be in progress. Just beyond the field was Jackson Park Creek, a gentle meandering stream where we fished for chub. In early spring when the ice broke up, this gentle stream could become a tyrant, often claiming the life of an unwary youngster.

In those days, after supper people would stroll - enjoying the cooler evening air. While strolling along the sidewalk, the custom was to stop and chat with the verandah people, sometimes joining them. Then the more senior boys would vacate their chairs for the company and take over the steps, leaving the tiny boppers to sit on the grass.

Mother would often make tea and she always had a supply of chewy hermit cookies on hand. In 15 minutes Mother could brew enough tea and serve enough hermits to sustain the Mormon Tabernacle Choir - both before and after the concert. This was neighbouring. This was verandah socializing. The conversation rarely touched on religion or politics, but centred around occurrences of local interest: how a neighbour was experiencing a bout of illness, how our baseball team was doing, how times were looking up, and they weren't. The spirit was optimistic. The kids kept quiet and listened.

Insp. James Reid of the City police, who lived on our street, would pass by nodding his "Good evening", and we knew by his presence that crime would never be a problem on our thoroughfares. Capt. William Jones of our fire department, once a member of the London Fire Brigade in England, would wave a greeting on his way past, ramrod straight, with every brass button gleaming, and we knew that in the event of a major conflagration, a steady hand would be at the throttle.

Miss Addy Doris, a music teacher who lived just up the street, would drop by. She taught piano to our entire family, but when it came to me she threw up her hands. Years later my mother told me that Addy's exact words were: "Katy, the lad has absolutely no talent. Perhaps when he's older he'll become a politician!"

Mrs. Tress Sheehan, who operated a boarding house on our boulevard, was a frequent verandah guest. She was, regrettably, childless. She really wasn't though: her boarders were her children, and there wasn't a kid on the block who wouldn't have cut off his arm for Tress. She was a truly special person who once in a while happens along - and I knew her, and she sat on our verandah!

One Sunday, Rev. John T. Finn, rector of St. Peter's Cathedral, while on his way to Mount St. Joseph for devotions, stopped at our house for a little verandah chat. Then having made this initial overture, he could hardly ignore the successive Catholic porches along the street. I'll bet he was late for vespers!

The nuns, hustling along Murray Street, en route from St. Peter's school to the mother-house, all knew my mom, and they would often stop and pass the time of day. One nun, whom my mother thought was truly special, happened to be my class teacher that year. I thought their friendship might give me a bit of an edge. However, the sister in her wisdom continued to regard me as something that had crawled out from under a damp plank.

Other neighbours would wander by: the Crarys, Loucks, Howdens, Maloneys, Burkes, Devlins and the contingent from Elm Street.

Miss Martha O'Donnell, about 100 years old (as I remember), would often fill a chair. It was great to see Martha in broad daylight, because if it were nighttime and she happened to catch me alone, she would tell me the most hair-raising ghost stories. Martha could have made a mint writing TV scripts.

On rainy afternoons, the verandah was the perfect refuge, where the younger kids played Snakes and Ladders or read comic books, the bigger boys read pulp detective or western stories, while the sisters were engrossed in hard-cover novels and, judging by their sad expressions, taking a hike in time with Louisa May Alcott.

Did you ever realize that brothers are the worst judges of the charms of their sisters? I never knew whether my two were the slightest bit attractive to the opposite sex or a couple of bow wows. However, they had no shortage of attention from young men. When one of the girls happened to be entertaining a chap late of an evening on the verandah, I would often spy on them. Nothing untoward ever happened. These sisters were either pillars of virtue, or the lads totally lacked initiative.

As the years passed and it became my turn to spark a young lass on the verandah late of an evening, I could be certain that one of my older brothers, defying fatigue, would sit with us - just for company. At 10 o'clock I would walk my girl home, hoping for better luck at the other end, only to find her father having a last pipe on their porch.

On Weller Street and Homewood Avenue, where the affluent people lived, verandas were different. They were broader, deeper, more heavily pillared. They had wooden bench swings suspended by heavy chains, grass matting on the floor, canvas deck chairs, wicker rockers and tables with potted plants - even wind chimes. Sometimes, part of the verandah would be enclosed with striped privacy awnings. I was told that in late afternoon, alcoholic beverages were served. Now, if this was true, and I'm not saying for a moment that it was, God only knows what else went on behind those gaily-striped privacy awnings.

In the older sections of our town, many verandas have been removed and replaced with tiny porches that couldn't accommodate two chairs, knee to knee. We are, however, seeing in newer subdivisions Victorian-style homes being built with sweeping verandas. Unfortunately, the residents know nothing of the necessary traditions.

I am going to visit 461 Murray Street and explain to the present owners that I was born on the kitchen table of that house, and I'll ask: "May I sit on your verandah this evening just for an hour or so? I won't be any bother. Look, I've even brought my own chair."

I will close my eyes and they'll be there: Tress Sheehan, Capt. Jones, Insp. Reid, all those great people. And Addy Doris - about those piano lessons, you should have hung in with me. I might have done you proud. Martha O'Donnell, it is dark out, but tell me one more ghost story. Really, I think I can handle it now.

I will speak about the scrub game going on across the way, which will lead to my wise comments about our local baseball team and how the infield needs new talent, and in my considered opinion, times are indeed looking up. They will all listen attentively, because I'm one of the white-heads now and it's my turn.

As for those people living in the new Victorian-style homes with their sweeping porches (who regrettably don't know what the hell to do with them), I offer my services. You must understand I am a graduate of verandah society and a walking authority on associated etiquette!

"I'll close my eyes, and they'll be there.'

Games We Used To Play

There is a tow-headed youngster down the road and we have become passing friends. The very young and the very old have always understood one another. Only we have difficulty in determining one another's age. I would put Tom at five, though I must be wrong because for three autumns, he has boarded the yellow phaeton bound for some distant seat of learning (en route passing nine schools to which he is ineligible, because he is from a different school zone).

I am quite sure Tom thinks I have hit the century mark. As we walk along the shoulder of the road, he always assumes the path of rougher proportion, lest I might lurch, take a dive, break into pieces, never to arise again. The topics of conversation are indeed wide-ranged. Is our prime minister "real"? Will the Leafs win the "Stanley Bucket" this year, defeat Russia in World Cup play, and each player have his sweater number retired in perpetuum at a civic sponsored dinner in tribute to the late Mr. Ballard? We confine our topics only to the very plausible.

Tom is bright and perpetually inquisitive. He prefaces his queries with: "Tell me, Mr. G., in the olden days...". This, of course, makes me want to break into song: "A glimpse of stocking was looked on as something shocking, now heaven knows, anything goes" - the lyrics accompanied by my very own soft-shoe routine. I refrain because there is a certain lady who keeps a sharp eye on all neighbourhood activities. Mine in particular! She is convinced I am an olive short of an acceptable martini. The lady wears a scapular around her neck, emblazoned with the numerals 911. Her ringed fingers never stray far from the blower. She is on the alert for any possibility. I further refrain because such bizarre behaviour would destroy the intellectual climate that exists between Tom and myself.

My young friend has a problem comprehending an existence minus TV and its sister VCR, munchies (or whatever that orange-coloured confection is so titled), an organized tadpole hockey league, or the absence of custom-fitted shoulder pads. His dad informed me as to the retail value of the lad's hockey equipment.

Automatically my mind flipped back to when those dollars would have provided for our family from late fall to mid-winter.

Over a period of time, I have convinced Tom that I did not spend my youth in a darkened Siberia, but really, really did have fun!

We took in an occasional movie at the Regent, watched our local Jays play baseball at Riverside, sleighed and tobogganed at Jackson Park and played hockey at free rinks. We listened to the Marconi, and caught Amos and Andy, and Arthur Tracey, the wandering street singer with his opener - "Marta, rambling rose of the wildwood" (you remember the gal with her fragrance divine). We thrilled when the sepulchral voice of Lamont Cranston murmured: "The shadow knows", followed by a strange, hollow "Ha, ha, ha." Today we would recognize that Mr. Cranston was a very sick person.

We felt our hair stand vertical and shifted closer to Mom as the squeaky door of "Inner Sanctum" opened to a nation of listeners. We heard Jack Benny, reputed to be close with the buck, being informed by Rochester that "You can't take it with you", and Mr. Benny responding: "If that's the case, then I'm not going."

We walked with Fred Allen down his alley, and met the folks. We listened as Edgar Bergen talked patiently to that little guy with the top hat, monocle and basswood head; and when George Burns attempted to understand Gracie's philosophies.

We waited all week for "Lux Radio Theatre"; never missed Clinton Bulhman in the morning, and at 2 p.m. on Sunday, made radio contact with Father Coughlin, broadcasting direct from the Church Of The Little Flower in Detroit, Michigan.

We played games: miggles, alleys, jack-knife, softball in the Albion Field (sometimes my brother would lend me his glove), run-sheep-run, potsy, kick-the-can, statues, hide-and-seek, chestnuts and battling tops. We built snow forts and had countless snowball fights. And last, but certainly not least, we played cowboys and Native people.

Girls, who were never good at anything, had their own games. They played jacks, May I?, tag, singing buttons (on a string), I Spy, hop-scotch on the sidewalk squares as they repeated "Step on a crack and you'll break your mother's back."

They also threw a sponge ball against a wall, caught it or tried to as they went through a silly ritual, singing standard lyrics like a Gregorian chant: "Ordinary, moving, laughing, talking, this hand, the other hand, this foot, the other foot, front clap, back clap, front-and-back, back-and-front, tweedle, twydle, curtsy, salute the flag, bow to the king - and roundabout." I believe this exercise gave birth to the expression: "Off the wall"!

Girls skipped incessantly, single rope or double Dutch, while they chanted things like "Tinker, tailor, soldier, sailor, rich man, poor man, beggarman, thief." When someone missed the rope, the name being called at the time they faultered indicated whom they would marry. They also chanted: "One, two, buckle your shoe - three, four, shut the door." And "Mabel, Mabel, set the table." Or "See-saw, Marjorie Daw." This is what girls did. Strange creatures. Hardly enough to keep the mind alive!

My young friend always listens attentively. At summer's end, he says: "Boy, you guys really had awesome times, didn't you?" Then Tom hustles up the road, not to be late for supper, or his favourite TV show.

I glance at my watch. If I go in right now, I'll catch the news. No! I'll stay right here and think about the games we used to play - in the olden days. Great games! Awesome! Radical!

courtesy Mary McCabe

Ron Cochrane - Ashburnham free rink, 1946.

courtesy Mary McCabe

Ashburnham free rink, 1946. Quaker Oats and Hunter street bridge in background.
Skaters: Ron Cochrane, Mary McCabe, Roy Barraclough, Pat Eggleton.

"In most neighbourhoods there was usually one woman everyone turned to for advice. My mom."

Pains, Potions And Elixirs Of The Past

This week, I received notification from the Ontario Ministry of Health that my OHIP premium payments would be eliminated. I am not sufficiently naive to think this a gift of the magi - someone must pay. However, it is reassuring. What comfort such legislation would have brought in the '30s! Then a doctor was summoned or consulted only under extreme circumstances - and the pronouncement: "We're going to have to get the doctor," struck terror in the heart of a child and caused financial concern for the parents.

The fields of surgery, the general practice of medicine and pharmacy are now highly sophisticated in comparison with yesteryear. Take my hand and walk back a few decades to the days of my youth, and we will examine how some health problems were resolved.

If you had a cold, a cough or a sore throat, a drop of turpentine on a spoonful of sugar, hot lemonade with honey, or a shot of Buckley's brought relief. A sock dampened with goose oil and wrapped tightly around the throat relieved discomfort. For chest congestion a mustard plaster was made: Water was added to dry mustard and the resultant paste was then spread on a cloth, covered by another cloth, and applied to your bare skin.

Frank McCarthy explained to me that in the event of a sore throat his mother would use a straw to blow sulphur down his throat. This resulted in a paroxysm of coughing, sneezing and choking. Just surviving the treatment gave one a sense of well-being.

If you had an itch caused by poison ivy, hives, nettles or chicken pox, you were plunged into a soda bath. For aching and sore muscles, a long soak in a bath of Epsom salts was prescribed.

Muscular afflictions were treated with Minard's liniment. Bert McLeod, a local druggist and sportsman, concocted a liniment that was widely used. Athletes insisted on McLeod's liniment; and Gunner Lynch, a trainer of some renown, endorsed it and used no other.

Bernie O'Toole told me of an uncle who, to ward off colds during the winter months, would heat coal oil on the kitchen stove and drink it. The trick, of course, was to drink it down before it burst into flame.

Every spring, my mother felt it necessary to give us a good clean-out. This was administered in the form of hot senna tea. Even now I gag at the thought of the taste. In winter there was no such thing as a vitamin supplement. Instead we received cod liver oil or the more palatable Scott's Emulsion. I can still see the bottle sitting on the shelf with the orange label showing a fisherman attired in a slicker and sou'wester, a big cod slung over his shoulder.

Vaseline or glycerine with rose water was rubbed into chapped hands and lips; Cuticura soap was used for pimples; yeast cakes were taken for acne, and bread poultices were applied to boils. A weak solution of peroxide prevented infection.

If you were tiny and had cut or scraped yourself, and your mom's kiss could not make it better, then out came the iodine, or the less painful red Mercurochrome - and then the Zam Buck or mecca ointment would be smoothed on the wound.

Irritations of the eye were treated with warm water and boracic acid (this should make your ophthalmologist shudder) and a sty was rubbed with a silver coin.

For irregularity or constipation, we were given Epsom salts or castor oil. Copeland's Sweet Castor Oil was easier to take. A recorded endorsement on the radio had a mother telling us: "My children drink it like water." Well, if such were the case, at least she always knew where the kids were! My grandmother contended that a sliver of Surprise soap inserted in the rectum would move mountains.

To get rid of hair lice, which I managed to pick up at school, my mother soaked my hair in coal oil, then she used a fine-tooth comb to remove the lice. She removed the bugs and part of my scalp as well, but at least I was socially acceptable to the other siblings.

My great aunt Sarah swore by Dr. Thomas's Electric Oil. It not only relieved symptoms, but actually cured coughs, colds, sore throats, catarrh, rheumatism, neuralgia, back problems, kidney disease and piles. In addition this oil could be used to treat similar maladies occurring in horses and cattle. We were amazed at how much of the elixir Sarah went through, but it did have an alcohol base and naturally was subject to rapid evaporation. Sarah is gone now - some liver problem.

Miss Alvina Mace of Ashburnham (you remember her) always recommended Northrop and Lyman's Beef, Iron and Wine Compound to counteract impurities of the blood and tune up the whole system.

Dr. Chase's Kidney and Liver Pills were on every bathroom shelf, and Lydia Pinkham's Pills were widely acknowledged as great stuff for the sometimes gentler sex plagued with periodic complaints.

In most neighbourhoods there was usually one woman everyone turned to for advice. If answers could not be found at this source, then the pharmacist was next in line. This gentleman was less intimidating than a physician and did not charge for a visit. Messrs. James Lynch, Frank Greatrix, John Nugent and Ernest Payne were fondly remembered in this role.

Do you recall when someone in the family had a contagious disease and your house was placed under quarantine - this fact advertised to the world by a placard nailed on the front door? The notices were different colours: blue for diphtheria, red for scarlet fever and white for whooping cough. With seven kids in our family, we sure spent a lot of time in quarantine. A maiden lady who lived near us always crossed the street as she approached our house.

When I was a youngster, I attended an outdoor medicine show. It took place north of McDonnel Street in an area bounded by Gilchrist, London and Donegal Streets, where they had a free rink in the winter. I remember the stage, and I remember the three girls wearing pink tights. There were acrobats, contortionists, dancers and musicians, and gosh they were grand! The doctor (the medicine man) had apparently abandoned a lucrative medical practice in Boston to live with the Shoshonean Indians and learn their secret of longevity. He introduced a chief of that nation who was 101 years old, though he appeared to be about 40 and was amazingly preserved and robust.

This elixir, the good doctor made available for the first time in Canada. The testimonials were numerous, undeniable and uncontestable. No matter what the ailment, the potion would seek it out and restore the fortunate person to health. Sales were brisk. Our next-door neighbour, who had been experiencing some physical decline, purchased three bottles. The medicine was effective. I can still hear him singing boisterously far into the night.

My brother, Fabian, suffered from asthma and was considered delicate - he had pneumonia four times. Dr. O'Reilly, who had his office at Hunter and Fleming Place, would rush to our house. It seemed it was always at night, and he and my mother would keep vigil at Fabian's bedside until he passed the crisis. Meanwhile, the rest of the family were on their knees downstairs saying the rosary and the litanies over and over again. Fabian displayed a remarkable tenacity for life and, with our spiritual intercession, reached adulthood and survived.

During the summer months I was obliged to spend a couple of weeks with my grandmother. This lady had an obsession with worms. She would explain in detail the difference between the thread worm of one-eighth to one-and-a-half inches in length, and the tape worm of sometimes 30 to 40 feet. Now that was enough to really blow a little kid's mind, and I imagined I could feel them snaking around inside me. Fortunately for my well-being, the matriarch possessed in her inventory a bottle of Mother Graves' Worm

Exterminator. I wondered how my mother could have been so negligent, so irresponsible, and gratefully swallowed down a generous portion. Holidaying with Grandma was not gangs of fun - but I never had worms, even to this day.

Since I grew up in an era when the prospect of an operation and being hospitalized could financially jeopardize a family, I truly appreciate the security of OHIP.

The Farmer's Almanac promises that this winter will be a harsh one, and I'm sorry that many of you will experience illness. I, myself, fortunately have an ace in the hole: two large bottles of Dr. Thomas's Electric Oil left to me as a legacy by good old Aunt Sarah.

My brother Elmer - "Up and over" - 1930s.

courtesy of Marlow Banks

Nassau Ski Meet 1938.

Summers - The Joys And Jeopardies

It is the last day of school and Sister begins the session as always. Then, about 11 a.m., she mentions the vacation months ahead, warns us about swimming in dangerous places, cautions us to look after one another. She tells us to remember our prayers, and occasionally to look at a newspaper to keep up with current events. Then she says that if we are very quiet, and go down the side stairs, she will let us out ahead of the other classes, because she considers this class — each one of us — special.

She is never disappointed. We charge down the stairs like a herd of elephants. I turn around. Sister smiles and waves. This is complete happiness.

Happiness, bliss, contentment imply an active or passive state of pleasure. Bliss is supreme delight. Contentment is a peaceful time of happiness. But I'm just a kid, and there are more than 60 days of summertime ahead of me - all the happiness, bliss and contentment I can handle.

We dam Jackson Park Creek, across the road and up the street from where I live. It is a wonderful swimming hole. Then a shore resident arrives on the scene, screams his head off, shakes his fist at us. He calls us hooligans. We aren't exactly sure what a hooligan is. He says we are flooding his property, interfering with the natural watershed, affecting the operation of the Lift Lock. We have to take the dam apart. Two weeks later he has a stroke and dies. After a few days, I ask his wife's permission to rebuild. She tells us to go ahead. I guess he had been screaming his head off at her most of his life. She comes to see what we are doing and offers suggestions, then gives us a bunch of rocks from the bottom of her garden. I tell her she can use the pool any time she wants.

One day my buddy and I are underneath the bridge spanning Jackson Park Creek at McDonnel Street. We are looking for turtles, and splitting a Turret cigarette. (Splitting is not just a part of being pals, smoking a whole one by myself would have made me throw up).

Adjacent to the Bonnerworth plant we see the drain pipe used by the mill to dump its waste dyes.

I say: "Let's climb up inside the pipe, and scare everybody in the joint."

My pal, whose IQ is on a level with mine, agrees.

I worm my way up about 10 feet, then I can't move any farther. I'm stuck. I'm soaked with perspiration, my right arm is in front of me, my left arm is pinned at my side. I'm panicking. Suppose they dump the dye now. Lord, I'll be killed. I'll be the weirdest corpse in the diocese - navy blue with orange splashes. People will come from miles around to see me. Grandma says I'll never amount to anything. She is wrong. Because of popular demand, the undertaker will refuse my family's request for a closed casket; I'll be written about in Liberty magazine. Grandma will read about me. I swear to God if I get out of here, I'll live the rest of my life in a bell jar. I manage to move my arm. I think my hand is bleeding. Something is trickling off it. It's sweat. I'm scared to death. I'm suffocating. I sweat so much I lubricate the pipe. I'm sliding! I'm out!

I'm crying and giggling at the same time. So is my pal. We pledge never to reveal what we have done. We are shaken, but we are happy. We split another Turret.

I learn to say the Confiteor in Latin, without hesitation. I feel I can sit on a park bench and rap away with Thomas Aquinas; and, if there is an embarrassing silence in the conversation, well, then, I'll just recite the Confiteor in Latin.

There is a good-looking girl visiting our neighbours. I finally get up the courage to ask her to go to the show with me. She'll say: "No", of course, but for once in my life, I'll dare to be a Daniel. My palms perspire when I ask her. She accepts immediately. I nearly drop dead. I say: "Swell." Later in the day I convince myself what a smooth operator I am.

We excavate a cave on the steep banks of Jackson Park Creek, big enough to seat three guys. The reading material is the *National Geographic*. It has pictures of native women wearing grass skirts and nothing else. You can see their BREASTS.

One night the cave collapses. We aren't there. A disaster like the Moose Creek Mine is averted. The *National Geographics* are lost forever in the cave.

One Sunday I'm confirmed. I become a soldier of Christ and take a third name - Joseph. I am the centre of attraction in the household for the first time.

A bunch of us go stealing rhubarb and apples in the heat of the night, and I am the first one to sound the alarm. "Run! Bright lights! The cops!" A fine way for a new soldier of Christ to behave! What gets into me? I think I have a natural talent for evil.

A chum and I climb up the inside of the 80-foot chimney of the deserted Hamilton foundry at Reid and Murray Streets. A third buddy watches from below for "jiggers" (our word for the police or anyone else who interferes with our pursuit of happiness).

I poke my head over the edge and see Reid Street, the spire of the cathedral, and the meandering course of Jackson Park Creek. The watcher below gets a bright idea. He starts a fire at the base of the chimney. We are alarmed. We struggle down the metal inserts, missing the odd one. We make it to the ground; choking and spitting, we emerge into the sunlight looking like two miniature Al Jolsons. We ignore the watcher; we bathe our faces in the creek.

I go home smelling like the hubs of hell. I have a bath. I wrap my shirt and cotton pants in newspapers, and put the evidence in the garbage.

Mother arrives home, glances at me in passing. Five minutes later she returns, takes my hand and says: "Tell me what happened." (All mothers are super-trained KGB operatives.)

I tell her the story. She stares in horror, then shouts: "Why are you trying to put me in an early grave?"

Then she embraces me, and says: "Okay, I won't tell Dad. But if you ever, ever do anything like that again, I'll kill you."

This, too, is another form of happiness - because mothers never really mean what they say.

There is a haunted house on Cross Street, right next door to the residence of a Mr. Meharry, who was murdered.

It is about 10 o'clock at night. I am with two friends. The dark clouds lower, then scud across the sky. A wind springs up, a patter of rain falls. The interior of the house is musty, dilapidated; part of the roof has fallen in.

Our flashlight throws yellowish images against the walls - and then the moans of some demented, tortured creature begin. We go out through the front door together on the dead run, three abreast.

The rain is now torrential. We run all the way to the lights of McDonnel and Park Streets. At the brightly lighted intersection in the pouring rain, we say goodnight.

Having a brush with dead spirits and getting away is wonderful happiness.

I watch the Orange Parade on the 12th of July. I know they are of a different persuasion (enemies, really), but the ladies are all in white, with big hats and coloured sashes. Somehow they remind me of Eleanor Roosevelt. Can you imagine a thousand Eleanors parading down George Street?

I am lying in bed at death's door. I have a summer cold. I think it is pneumonia. My family is away, with the exception of one sister. The priest should be notified. The sister is not unsympathetic. She prepares a mustard plaster (her first) and puts it on my chest. I awaken in the middle of the night, just in time to remove the plaster before it eats completely through my body, and the mattress, and the floor below. In the morning, except for third degree burns, I feel better.

I neck for the first time. I kiss a girl square on the mouth, then lie awake half the night remembering how she tasted, smelt. I wonder if this constitutes lust, one of the seven deadly sins, or maybe God doesn't start counting until you are 12. In which case I still have two months of total abandonment. A happy thought!

I take long hikes in the country, sometimes by myself. One day I see a cow standing near the fenceline. What is she doing? My God, she is having a baby! I've never seen anything like this in my life. In books they say you should boil water, get a kettle. There is no one around. I stand transfixed. Bossy does her thing, cleans up the calf, and looks at me as if to say: "It's okay, Sport. Get a grip on yourself." I've been exposed to one of the mysteries of life. I'm happy.

I get my first bicycle. It is blue and has somewhat thicker tires than usual. I buy it at Banks Bicycle Shop and Mr. Banks tells me it is "top of the line". I have the handlebars turned backward, because that is what guys do. At night, when I am in bed, I worry about it. Sometimes I sneak downstairs to look out in the backyard and see if my bicycle is okay. I buy a security chain, then two security chains, then lose both keys. I spend one entire Saturday morning with a hacksaw, removing the chains.

I go fishing. The end of my bamboo pole bends over like a scimitar, and I know I have caught the biggest bass in Canadian waters - big enough to feed the family at supper on Friday.

The day is scorching. I'm sitting on the front verandah steps. The ice wagon comes down the street. I run after it, grab a handful of shards, then sit in the shade sucking on the ice, spitting out the sawdust and picking out the soft wood slivers underneath my fingernails that I got from the corrugated wooden floor of the wagon.

I go to the Conklin midway at the exhibition grounds. There are throngs of people - the carnies, a different kind of people. I watch the games of chance, the carrousel with its familiar music, the Ferris wheel, the new rides, twice more dangerous this year than last, girls in grass skirts from some exotic island, the "Thin Man", the "Fat Lady", the mysteries behind the canvas of the side shows. There are raucous sounds, strange smells. This is life and it pulsates.

Sunday after Mass we have dinner - all nine of us. We have dinner at noon and supper at 6 o'clock. My father goes over the sermon of the day, in the possible event we missed the message. After dinner, my dad and I walk to St. Peter's cemetery, a distance of about 28 miles, or so it seems to me. We visit the graves of family and friends. I like the cemetery, and I wander around reading all the epitaphs and saying prayers for the repose of the soul, if I recognize a name.

You see, happiness is often very private - a question of taste and attitude.

Happiness just IS!

"And I was twelve years old."

courtesy of Marlow Banks

"I get my first bicycle. I buy it at Banks Bicycle Shop and Mr. Banks tells me it is top of the line."

Clare and Bette (the chatelaine). Photograph taken for 40th wedding anniversary.

I Remember My Uncle Ronald

I only met my uncle Ronald twice in all the days of my life. Yet I can close my eyes and there he is.

Ronald was the youngest of 11 children on the paternal side - an old Ennismore family. During the First World War he was a defector - refusing to serve in the military and, with others, hid out.

In small Irish-Canadian communities, such an attitude was not unique. The idea of fighting a war for England was not a hip, hip hurrah prospect. There was a floating bridge linking Ennismore with the mainland, in fact it was the longest of this design in the world. When Sir Sam Hughes' military police were observed crossing the bridge, the word was quickly passed along to "The Cross", the social and commercial heart of the hamlet. Then the whistle of the Myrtle Cheese Factory would sound three long blasts to alert the boys to find sanctuary in their "Sherwood Forest".

In 1918 the government promised amnesty for those who surfaced. Those who did were quickly hustled into uniform, given a modicum of training and shipped overseas.

By the time Ronald arrived over there, armistice had been declared. Once back home, having seen some of the brighter lights, Ronald was no longer content with the coal oil lamps of the ancestral farmhouse. He left Canada and went to Chicago, where he spent much of his lifetime.

On his occasional visits home, I had the opportunity to study him. He was a man of slight build, fair hair and complexion, with a gentle manner, somewhat reminiscent of the actor Leslie Howard. Immaculately attired in a tan tropical suit and coordinating Panama hat, he appeared affluent.

Ronald's posture left a lot to be desired. Mother later informed me that, hiding in a rain barrel behind the barn to avoid the military, was not conducive to a "shoulders back" stance. I feel most of us can relate to this. Well, at least those who have spent any significant time in a rain barrel.

There was something else that I observed - a noticeable bulge in the left breast of his jacket. Ronald was carrying "a piece"! If you attended a separate school, as I did, you notice those things.

I know chaps like Sylvester Stallone who can walk through doors without opening them - sure they're heavy, but it's the little guys who are the real pistols.

For the next decade nothing was heard of my uncle. The family entertained the possibility of amnesia. I speculated that perhaps Ronald had cast a lascivious eye on the kid sister of the boss and Big Al had had him waxed; or perhaps George "Bugs" Moran had been offended, Frank "The Enforcer" Nitti, miffed. In those interesting times in the toddling town, if you lacked a proper knowledge of social decorum, you could well be part of the salmon run up the Chicago drainage canal. Then again, Ronald could have copped a plea, and was doing eight to 10 in Joliet.

Eureka! Ronald resurfaced - still the tailor's dummy, still that mild and gentle manner and now wearing horn-rimmed glasses. I felt a pang of sympathy and alarm. In that business, if your eyes go, it can spell trouble. I looked, but there was no bulge in the suit jacket, however, a small briefcase was always at his side, just a palm away. No explanation was offered re the 10-year hiatus, the odd query was parried skilfully.

I never saw my Uncle Ronald again. I continued to subscribe to the *Police Gazette*, the weekend *Tribune*, and pored over the pages. There was no correspondence with the immediate family. A maiden aunt would receive the occasional note or postcard saying only: "The weather is indeed salubrious."

The years passed by - 10, 20, 30. Then one January morning, I received a phone call from Monsignor McNulty of St. Petersburg, Florida, to advise me that Uncle Ronald had passed away early that morning, his death, peaceful. Thank God! In my mind's eye, I could see the mattresses, the shoot-out, the resultant publicity.

The funeral service could be delayed if I was able to attend. It was impossible. Then I recalled that a sister and some of her family were vacationing in the area. I gave the cleric their address. He assured me that he would make a personal visit "to soften the blow."

I immediately tried to contact my sister to alert her to the circumstances and her forthcoming visitor, to counteract the possibility of her blurting out, "Uncle who?" The circuits were busy.

Two hours later my telephone rang, and the salutation was: "You idiot, why didn't you call me?" The dialogue with the priest was as I had anticipated.

According to the original conversation with the monsignor, Ronald was not only his parishioner, but a close friend. He had lived some years in a pleasant guest home in St. Pete's. He was a quiet man, well thought of, attended Mass every morning (some of the shooters get the call late in life).

I questioned my niece, a reasonably astute young woman who had attended the funeral service. Had she noticed any stretch limos, any vulgar floral displays, guys in tuxedos? Negative on all three counts. Could I have been wrong about my uncle all those years, when in reality he was just a quiet man, one of those private individuals? It was unlikely, with all I knew about him.

A fortnight later I called the monsignor explaining that I was, of course, fully aware of the life and times of Ronald Galvin, but there were a few things, and if he would be kind enough... . There was a long pause and then a chuckle and I knew he was a product of one of the more enlightened seminaries of the rebel states. "Yes!"

Ronald was a private person, a former minor executive of Northern Electric in Chicago, active in affairs of the church, involved in a madrigal singing group of the same town, most interested in the study of certain flora of the eastern and southern seaboard, which he photographed. Many of his truly treasured photos he carried with him in a small briefcase ... . Hot damn! You think you have somebody all figured out! The subscription to the *Police Gazette* and the yellowed copies of the *Tribune* now gather dust in the attic.

You know what? Some day, I promise, I will go to St. Pete's, visit his grave, buy a floral wreath, the big vulgar horseshoe type, and the ribbon will read: "Good luck, Uncle Ronald." Just like the shooters get.

He'd get a bang out of that, and I'd feel better, too!

Clare autographs "My Town - My Memories" at book launch, Sunday, September 12, 1993 - with sister Cleta Murphy and brother Doug.

H

I

J

K

L

M

N

O